A TORBAY CENTURY

An illustrated history by John Pike
Photographs compiled by Mike Thompson

A TORBAY CENTURY

An illustrated history by John Pike
Photographs compiled by Mike Thompson

breedon **books**
PUBLISHING

First published in Great Britain in 2003 by
The Breedon Books Publishing Company Limited
Breedon House, 3 The Parker Centre,
Derby, DE21 4SZ.

ISBN 1 85983 344 6

Printed and bound by Butler & Tanner,
Frome, Somerset, England.

Cover printing by Lawrence-Allen Colour Printers,
Weston-super-Mare, Somerset, England.

Contents

Preface

MOST of the histories published recently take the three Torbay towns – Torquay, Paignton and Brixham – and relate their stories individually. All three are proud of their identity and when they were amalgamated as Torbay in 1968, it was not with total approbation by many residents, particularly those living in Brixham. However, many aspects of life around the Bay have had common elements over the past century – and much longer in some instances. This book will attempt here to link these together and show our common heritage. The *Centenary History of Torquay* was a limited-edition book, published in 1992, that presented the history of just one of the three towns and told its story with the help of well-chosen pictures. Its success was very much due to the help given to the Centenary Committee by the *Herald Express*. Its involvement here is even greater and its name appears on the title-page.

Stories in local newspapers do much to make history 'a good read'. Torbay is fortunate to have had weeklies dating back over a century and a half. From being just a list of residents, the *Torquay Directory* became a newspaper in 1839, covering national, international and local news. The dispatches from the American Civil War battlefields make fascinating reading. In 1915 George Bernard Shaw was given over 20 column-inches for his letter to the editor. The *Torquay Times* came on the scene in 1865 and had a number of distinguished editors. George Lidstone, it last owner and editor, played a major role in creating news stories both in words and pictures. Regrettably neither of these weeklies has survived. The *Herald Express* was the result of a merger between the *Torbay Express* and *Torbay Herald*, both evening dailies, started in the early 1920s. The *Express* had an editor in the 1930s, 40s and 50s who made a major impact on local affairs, Reginald A. Colwill. His 'Idler' column was written daily by hand and its publication was awaited eagerly by his followers. As it approached the 75th anniversary of publication, the *Herald* entered the new technological age with a website that can be accessed by the world.

Picture Acknowledgements

Much of the success of *Herald Express* 'Bygones' over the years has been due to the willingness of various individuals and organisations to lend items from their collections for publication.

For this book the principal source was, of course, the archives of the *Herald Express* and we are also indebted to Torquay Museum, helpful as ever, for images from its comprehensive pictorial records.

The author's own collection was naturally utilised, while other important contributions came from local postcard collectors David James of Brixham, Leslie Retallick of Torquay and, most significantly, David Mason, the enthusiastic and knowledgeable chairman of Torbay Postcard Club. By making their collections available in this way, postcard collectors play a vital role in enriching the appreciation of local history and widening our awareness of Torbay's heritage.

Introduction

JUST before the Imperial Hotel was built in the mid-19th century, the *Torquay Directory* reported: 'It has long been felt that Torquay, with a large, wealthy and increasing population, and a great number of visitors who resort to it in both winter and summer for health and pleasure, stands much in need of the accommodation of a first-class modern hotel of the character so successfully established in London and some of the leading watering places of England and on the Continent'. As the 20th century opened, the Imperial was still in great demand. Built in a most prestigious position, its windows looked south over an unspoilt Torbay.

In January 1905 Sir Henry Irving, the first actor to have accepted a knighthood, stayed there for several weeks. When he left he affirmed that his stay had been 'in one of the choicest spots in the world'.

An early Torquay marketing slogan read: 'The general effect of the white houses, the grey limestone cliffs, and the foliage and greensward forming the ground to the whole, is unusually picturesque and calculated to soothe as far as scenery can soothe, the lassitude and depression of ill-health'. By 1900 fit and healthy potential customers, rather than the invalids, were being targeted. The message today is even more simple. A recent English Riviera guide promised that 'you don't have to go abroad for sun, sea and something special. It's all here – all the year round.'

Over the decades millions of visitors have accepted the invitation – and we hope they will continue to do so!

Setting the scene – the panorama of Torbay

TORBAY the place comprises three towns – Torquay, Paignton and Brixham. For some years Torquay's northern boundary was near Shaldon, a strip of land from St Marychurch having been acquired by the Corporation in 1935. When the County Borough of Torbay was created in 1974 this land passed to the newly-formed Teignbridge District Council. The walk beside the sea remains unspoiled still and with the whole of Torbay to the south, is part of the South West Coast Path. The publication of the *South West Coast Path through Torbay* by the Torbay Coast and Countryside Trust is a fascinating introduction to wildlife around the Bay. It tells in full colour the history of the coast and

The Natural Arch rock formation near Torquay harbour was a favourite spot for tourists. This view is from a postcard mailed in 1912 with a Babbacombe franking mark and the message: 'Dear Miss Ida, Just a line from "Sunny (?) Devon". They call this arch "London Bridge" and we also have down here Fleet Street and the Strand – so you see we feel quite at home…'

This view from above the harbour shows how the Torquay waterfront looked around 1890. Land had to be reclaimed from the waters of the bay before Torquay could have the extra space for its Princes Gardens and a Promenade going towards Torre Abbey Sands. Below: The view looking the other way as the 20th century began, with the new Princess Gardens prominent on the seafront. Bottom: Work going on in the 1930s reclaiming more land from the bay in order to extend the Promenade and build the sunken gardens leading from Princess Pier to Abbey Sands.

describes the birds and animals that inhabit both land and sea. Names given to inlets and coves by our ancestors are now well-known locations and are recorded on its maps: Herring and Mackerel Coves at Maidencombe; Smugglers Hole and Roundhouse Point at Petitor; Black Head and Brandy Cove at Babbacombe; Fairy Cove at Paignton; Saltern and Shell Coves and Armchair Rock at Broadsands; Silver and Ivy Coves at Churston and, on the Channel coast at Brixham, Cod Rock, Durl Head and St Mary's Bay.

We are told that the cliffs provide a lesson in geology. At St Marychurch the red sandstones and grey limestones lie side by side. The limestone survives better than its neighbour. With global warming, there are forecasts of changes to sea levels; this is unlikely to have much impact on the Babbacombe Bay coastline but the increased rainfall has already caused the cliffs here to crumble into the sea. Daddyhole Plain is also of limestone (there is still evidence of the quarrying that ended many years ago); this includes the Natural Arch. The strata of the rock runs almost vertically, and the action of the sea over the centuries has produced the lofty opening clearly visible from Haldon Pier and elsewhere. At Corbyn Head the soft red sandstone has weathered rapidly. Less than 200 years ago there were two arches; now both have gone.

Humans have had their

Corbyn Head in Torquay was given to the town in 1907; this post-war view shows the magnificent elm trees which were later destroyed by Dutch Elm Disease.

Torquay's new Promenade and sunken gardens, completed in 1934.

impact on the coastline too. Until the 19th century the only way from Torquay harbour to Cockington and Paignton was a tortuous inland route past Torre Church. The coastal road under Waldon Hill was of relatively simple construction. A strong stone wall was built on the sands and the space behind it filled with rock and soil. In this way the New Road (now Torbay Road) was constructed under Waldon Hill and in front of Torre Abbey. The same principle was used again in the 1890s when building the Princess

Gardens. On this occasion a second wall was built on the harbour floor and a vast amount of infill put in between the new and old walls. In the early 1930s Torquay Corporation widened the promenade between the Pier and Torre (or Tor, as it has sometimes been known) Abbey Sands. The method adopted was somewhat different. The work was started by steel-piling on the sands when the tide was out. Later a stone wall was built behind the piles and the new promenade created on the reclaimed land. The paths and sunken gardens look little different now. The proposal to put a Beach Centre adjacent to the Torre Abbey Sands slipway brought complaints from the hotels nearby and the scheme was put 'on hold' in October 1997. Eventually the go-ahead was given and the rather ponderous-looking structure was completed in June 1998.

Corbyn Head was given to the town in 1907 by Richard Mallock's trustees. There was a two-gun battery on the Head during World War Two. These were 4in Japanese weapons dating from the earlier conflict. The armaments were never fired in anger but there was a serious accident at the battery on 11 August 1944 during a test shooting in front of Army top brass. Four men, some of whom were Home Guards, died instantly. Two more died later.

For many years there was on the Head a row of magnificent mature elm trees that grew ever more majestic. These were among the thousands infected by Dutch Elm Disease in the 1970s. Before it struck there were between 750,000 and a million trees of all sorts within Torbay's boundaries. By 1981 some 90 per cent of the elms had gone, this avenue being among those cut down: the view to the south had changed forever.

By 1900 Paris Singer, son of American millionaire Isaac, owned much of Preston. Four years later he announced that he had a plan to erect 'excellent marine residences on both sides of the road' on his Redcliffe Estate. The properties were built on the landward side of what is now Marine Drive, and instead of doing the same thing on the rough ground on the seaward side, he offered the land to the town for just £600 an acre. Some acres of foreshore were later added to the offer and the whole became the public open space we know as Preston Green. Further development was delayed by World War One. The Green, however, did play its part in the war effort, being used for military training and trench digging. Levelling of the area started in 1920 and by 1924 the promenade, shelters and tennis courts had been completed. Further improvements were made in 1931 and 1939 but its appearance today is little changed from its heyday in the 1930s. The prestige block of flats behind the high wall at the south end date from 1986.

'Paega's tun', later becoming the more familiar Paignton, was an ancient settlement built on the first firm ground behind the marsh. The water-level is still close to the surface and when Paignton library was built on the last piece of marshy ground, special pumps were needed to raise waste water and sewage up to the correct level.

The town of Paignton has always been proud of the wide open space behind the sands. Covenants state 'that no dwelling house or other building other

The approach to Goodrington's South Sands, perhaps in the late 1930s, showing the South Sands café.

Holidays under canvas at Goodrington between the wars.

a bed at Dartmouth' and was personally responsible for turning the large house into sick quarters. Young's Park nearby became an Urban Protection Area in 1996 and more recently, in 1999, the Seashore Centre was opened at Drake House.

At Saltern Cove there are Upper Devonian slatey shales and red mudstones. Fossils have been found there but the area is now a protected marine nature reserve.

than that needed for shelter or recreation… shall be erected or built upon the said piece of land' and 'that it be kept in order for use as, and for a public park and ground for recreation for ever'. However, this failed to prevent the erection of the Festival Theatre in 1967, or the huge Apollo Cinema that has replaced it.

Goodrington's two large sandy beaches, North Sands and South Sands, achieved great accessibility between the wars. Purchases of land began to be made in 1913 and there was a great boost to Goodrington's popularity when the Great Western Railway opened Goodrington Sands Halt in 1928. This was a new destination for day-trippers from all over Devon. It was during this work behind North Sands that a local legend was dispelled. The bottomless May's Pool, whose alleged existence had so worried the railway-builders a century earlier, was found not to exist at all. The Cliff Gardens and Promenade at the north end was opened in 1931.

The story of the new Goodrington we see today started with the purchase of the Goodrington Hotel in October 1973 by Torbay County Borough Council from Mount Charlotte Investments for £450,000. It took some years before the land could be redeveloped. The Water Park, with its pale green curves and twists was first opened in 1989. What is today the Inn on the Quay was a naval hospital in Napoleonic times. The seamen of the day owed a great debt to Dr Thomas Trotter, Surgeon to the Fleet, who often visited HM ships anchored in the Bay. He objected to sick sailors being 'two-by-two in

Paignton Council's progressive policy towards extending its ownership of the coastline continued right up until 1939. The strip of land from Goodrington to Broadsands and the foreshore was bought in 1931 (the latter for £207). Later, in 1938, the headland at Three Beaches was purchased. The acquisition of the open land at Broadsands was still under negotiation when war broke out: it was finally bought in 1948 (by then prices had risen and the 115 acres cost £43,000). The Crown lease of the foreshore at Broadsands and Elberry was purchased in the same year. Waterside Camp, just behind the Sands, was bought by the Council in 1939; it was described as then being the only municipally-owned camp in Britain.

Sixty years ago Broadsands was a wide open beach. After the fall of France in 1940 an elaborate 'forest' of steel poles was erected to keep German troops from landing. In view of their flimsy construction, it is doubtful if they would have kept the enemy at bay for long. Subsequently the beach and the nearby Elberry Cove were developed with a large car park in close proximity. As part of this development, a small café complex was completed in time for the 1973 season.

One story, untold at the time because of the rigidly-enforced press censorship, concerns the field behind Broadsands. A United States Air Force B17-bomber force-landed there at the end of 1942. The ground around the aircraft was said to be littered with oranges. Apparently it was flying back from North Africa when it ran out of fuel. The bomb-load of fruit was intended for sale to fellow-airmen at the crew's home base.

Battery Gardens at Brixham takes the name from the Napoleonic Wars or even earlier. Its superb position overlooking the whole of the Bay made it ideal for positioning guns for the defence of the realm. In the early 1940s a modern battery was built. It had two 4.7in gun batteries concealed in the hillside below with an observation post, searchlights and a Bofors anti-aircraft gun above. The post has survived and in early 2002 a group of enthusiasts were able to open it to the public as a heritage site.

Stone from Berry Head was used for the fort built at the time of the Napoleonic scare in the late 18th century. At the start of the 20th century Trinity House erected a lighthouse which became known as the smallest, highest and deepest light in the British Isles, requiring no further elevation than that given by the headland itself. Its beam is visible many miles out to sea. For many years it was acetylene gas that worked the mechanism and provided the light (and was very reliable) but this was replaced by electricity in 1994. The *Herald Express* reported: 'The lighthouse has undergone a major overhaul and is now operated by a single 60-watt lamp. It is powered by two electric motors and if one fails, the other operates. The equipment switches on and off by an electronic device which measures the ultraviolet light from the sun'.

Quarrying continued on the landward side until about 30 years ago and, when plans to extend the workings were announced, it seemed as

A fine view of Paignton Green in the 1950s, showing the entertainment marquee almost opposite the end of Torbay Road.

though the whole Head would be destroyed. However, in 1969 Torbay Council (as it had recently become) bought the whole headland and shortly

Paignton's Festival Theatre under construction in 1967.

afterwards it was designated a Country Park and Nature Reserve. Subsequently a Visitor Centre was erected beside Fort No 1.

A CCTV camera, mounted on the cliffs adjacent, records the activities of seabirds nesting on the cliffs. There are rare and threatened wildflowers, including Goldilocks Aster, growing here. These, and others, have the opportunity to flourish in the mild climate and exposed conditions. One of the creatures that enjoys the undeveloped countryside, particularly around Maidencombe, is the cirl bunting. We are told that a decade ago there were fewer than 700 birds breeding in the whole country; today there are 1,000 and numbers are still rising.

Sharkham Point, on the other side of St Mary's Bay, is an open park through which the South West Coast Path runs. Its rugged beauty today is due to a fairly recent 'face-lift'. For many years iron ore was mined. There was also a profitable export industry of red and brown haematite for smelting and for paint manufacture. In 1930 an official report noted that 'the mines are now disused but there are traces of old shafts, adits and ore refuse'. It continued: 'Between 1858 and 1914 300,000 tons were mined here, some went to South Wales for smelting, some was used on ships'. For years Brixham Urban District Council used the land as the town refuse tip. Refuse vehicles used the narrow access road throughout the day from early morning. Seagulls congregated there in great numbers.

A decade or so ago, however, the area was restored with great care to its original state. Wild creatures now breed there undisturbed.

Evidence of the old sea level can be found at various points around the coast. Known sometimes as raised beaches, these platforms show evidence of

In recent years the old gun emplacements and observation post in Battery Gardens at Brixham have been opened up as a heritage site in a campaign spearheaded by a group of volunteers who also established a small heritage centre museum on the road down to Fishcombe Cove. Pictured here is the observation post on its re-opening day. The museum was opened by former Brixham pilot Captain Bob Curtis in December 2002.

an earlier beach level – sand, shingle and marine shells. At Hope's Nose there is one eight metres above present sea level; and another at Sharkham which is about five metres above high water mark. These rarities date mostly from the glacial period, 25,000 years ago or earlier.

The importance of limestone for improving the land has been known for hundreds of years. The amount of the stone quarried locally can be judged from a survey some years ago that showed there were 374 lime-kilns in Devon at one time of which over 200 were on the South Coast. One fine example still exists beside Galmpton Creek; it looks much as it did a century or more ago.

Miles of beaches – from Watcombe to Man Sands

JUST as the 20th century dawned, a major step was taken in Torbay. Mixed, or 'continental', bathing as it was sometimes called, was permitted for the first time. In one sense, the local authority had the last laugh, as the concession applied only from 1 October 1900, long after the bathing season had come to an end. However, the innovation did not quite see the end of bathing machines. Though a Paignton guidebook commented: 'The modern bather does not want to be towed down to the waters so as not to be seen entering or leaving the water. They may have served some purpose in the Victorian era, today they have neither the merit of ornament nor utility'. The machines continued to be used on Paignton Sands and there was a row in use at Oddicombe until at least 1910.

Maidencombe and Watcombe, Torbay's two northernmost beaches, were little used until the 1920s when motor-buses started to run out from Torquay town centre. Access was difficult both for bathers (the path was rough and steep) and lessees of the beach rights (who had to bring all their gear around by boat from Babbacombe). As late as 1930 the rent was only £30 a year. Until the summer of 2002 this was the only privately-managed beach in Torbay. It took a County Court action by the Authority to regain possession.

For many years Oddicombe consisted of crystal white pebbles, quite different from all the other beaches around Torbay. The answer to this phenomenon lay in the existence, across the bay, of Long Quarry. For two centuries or more the beach was fed with stone which dropped overboard from the loading vessels and was carried over the bay by storm and tide. The end of quarrying caused the beach to disappear and in recent times lorry-loads

The Babbacombe cliff railway takes another load of passengers down to the waterside, with a busy 1960s Oddicombe beach in the background, complete with pleasure boat at the pontoon.

Changing styles in beach huts in Torquay – the trio at Anstey's Cove (centre) look very plain, while the ones beneath the elms at Corbyn Head are at least two-toned and those at Oddicombe beach (top) have their distinctive pointed roof.

Herald Express concluded: 'Although contractors have removed the loose rock, following an earlier fall, there is still the possibility of further ones'.

As we have seen, for many years men and women bathed at separate ends of the beach – never together. However, one of the last acts of the St Marychurch councillors (just before the parish became part of Torquay) was to approve mixed bathing – just a few months before its larger neighbour did so. There was a great boost to the beach prosperity in 1924 when the National Electric Construction Company decided to build a cliff railway. This opened two years later The gradient was 2.84, the track 720ft (221 metres) and it took 12 men some 15 months to complete the task. In 1934 the Torquay Corporation bought the railway and have been the operators ever since. It closed down during World War Two, was rebuilt in 1950 and in the 1960s was carrying 750,000 passengers to and from the beach each year. A recent major overhaul, including relaying the track and building new cars, means that it can continue to fill the beach for many years to come. Henry Thomas leased the beach, owned the bathing tents, the deckchairs and even the boats that were for hire. As late as 1936 he was paying the Corporation just £500 for the season. Not long afterwards the whole operation passed into municipal hands – and the council has been running it ever since.

of old building materials have had to be dumped to rebuild it.

In March 1925, the *Torquay Directory*, reporting a landslip, said: 'Other parts of the cliff are extremely dangerous and likely to fall at any moment'. The problem continues. In July 2001 warning notices were put up and the western end roped off. The

Anstey's Cove in the days when it was owned by the Thomas family, whose notice written in Latin above the door became well known.

The Thomas family sign at Anstey's Cove, with the lines which conclude: 'Thomas is the man who provides everything, And also teaches young people to swim'.

Connected to Oddicombe by a seaside path is Babbacombe Beach. Its picturesque appearance complete with small fishing boats has attracted photographers, professional and amateur, since the earliest days. In spite of its associations with John 'Babbacombe' Lee, 'the man they could not hang', it has never been a major tourist attraction. It was used mainly by fishermen right up until the 1930s. The access road is steep and winding, more suitable for hill-climbs than holiday drivers. Its picture postcard appearance disappeared forever when the promenade was rebuilt in the 1970s. The small harbour for the fishermen was erected by subscription many years ago. In 2003 its condition was causing concern.

Just around the headland is Anstey's Cove. Owned by the Thomas family until 1929, it has always been popular as a bathing beach. At one time a noticeboard stood beside the lane above the beach. It began:

"Picnics supplied with hot water and tea
At a nice little house down by the sea"

However, what the board did not say was that the Cove had been a well-known landing-place for the local smugglers. A smuggling episode in 1850 had excited the newspapers of the day but it was the capture in October 1988 that filled the front pages of

Sand sculptor and former soldier Daniel Anning stands by his work on Abbey Sands in Torquay. He was a well known sight in the 1920s and 1930s, though he had been working on the sands even before World War One. This depiction of a tiger fighting with a lion was one of his most famous creations and was called 'A Battle Royal', with underneath the inscription: 'Only a poor man trying to earn a trifle'.

the *Herald Express.* Some 60 police officers and customs men lay in wait in the woods and in the grounds of the Palace Hotel nearby. Operation Kleese was in progress. The *Etoile de Lisieux*, a converted trawler, was anchored off the beach and the watchers waited until a small inflatable dinghy had unloaded her cargo – and then they pounced. At the time of the trial in Exeter the full scale of the seizure was revealed: 70 bales of cannabis resin worth over £4 million had been recovered. Some had been throw overboard and had to be trawled up from the sea bed. Alain Quessaud, the skipper of the trawler and Ken Massey were both found guilty and given long prison sentences. Eight others had pleaded guilty; they also received long sentences. It was truly a case of history repeating itself. If the culprits had researched any of the history books they would have realised that as well as being a smugglers' landing spot, it was also where others more experienced than they, in similar circumstances, had been apprehended.

Just as popular to smugglers as Anstey's Cove was Redgate Beach on the other side of the low rocks. For many years access to it was, on the south side, up a rickety ladder. In 1930 a bridge was built and the new Redgate Beach was formally opened in June 1931. However, in early 1998 a series of cliff-falls forced its closure. There are indications that it may never be reopened.

Meadfoot Beach looks serene and peaceful unless a south-easterly gale is blowing. Like other Torbay beaches there have been several landslips there. A look at a 1920s photograph shows the scale of the problem. In 1930 the road surface in St Mark's Road

was cracking so badly the owner of the end house, The Mount, was concerned that it, too, might slide down on to the beach. These fears were happily unfulfilled – and with the solid 100-metre-long promenade now keeping the waters at bay, all is well. Midway along the beach was the Meadfoot Spring and throughout the 1930s Torquay Corporation bottled its waters. The Medical Officer reported that because of the water's high purity, it could be compared with the French Evian and Vittel waters and would thus relieve rheumatism, gout, bladder, gastro-intestinal and metabolic disorders. In 1938 a proper scientific analysis was conducted which confirmed that it contained magnesium, calcium and bicarbonates. A small bottling hut was erected and two sizes were offered, one of them selling at 2s (10p) for a dozen bottles that could be sent to any address in the United Kingdom. The attractively-labelled bottles were sold over the counter at the Marine Spa, in local hotels and chemist shops. After World War Two the water was found to be polluted and could no longer be drunk. However, as late as 1974 the *Sunday Independent* reported that an Exeter doctor collected all his water from the spring and advised his patients to do likewise. Some time later the stream was diverted into a sealed culvert and can now no longer be traced.

A Typhoon fighter aircraft of the RAF made a forced-landing on the rocks below the Meadfoot wall in May 1943. The pilot was uninjured and a recovery party from Exeter soon had the damaged plane on a Queen Mary low-loader.

Dancers from a Festival Theatre show enjoy themselves on Paignton beach in 1972, no doubt for newspaper publicity.

John Stafford with his Punch and Judy show on Paignton beach in 1965. 'Stafford's Royal Punch & Judy' is the legend above the stage.

Bathing Machines near the Inn

Beacon Cove is said to be the oldest in Torquay, the first bathing machine being for hire there in 1807. It was for many years known as the Ladies Bathing Cove. Tents later took the place of the machines and the Cove was popular with families. In late Victorian times the RNLI stationed one of its lifeboats at the Cove. After the craft's removal in March 1923, the boat-house became a café, serving thousands of drinks and ice-creams to the many residents and visitors who flocked there.

Torre Abbey Sands has been enjoyed for generations both by residents and visitors. Its firm red sands remain so because it is washed thoroughly twice daily by the ebb and flow of the tide.

The widening of Torbay Road in the early 1930s meant the end of Daniel Anning's sand-sculptures. Mr Anning was an unemployed World War One veteran. He created his work in the wet sand (the 'Bengal Tiger' was his most famous, but he created also a statue in sand to 'Dr Cook, North Pole Explorer'). It survived only an hour or so – the incoming tide forcing both workman and artist to retreat from the waves.

In September 1942 a German pilot in a ME109 fighter-bomber crashed on Abbey Sands after being shot down by a local machine-gunner. Although the beach itself was not mined, access to it was denied by barbed-wire and other defences. A policeman could only watch helplessly from the Torbay Road as the plane was engulfed in flames and its occupant, Pilot Unteroffizier W. Hofer, burned to death.

A good-sized crowd watches the Punch and Judy show at Preston beach in the 1960s. In the background is the Redcliffe Hotel.

Children enjoy the paddling pool at Young's Park, Goodrington, in the 1960s.

Council refused to allow any stalls to be put up on the Sands. However, it relented three years later and tenders were invited to sell sweets. Rights to do so were granted to three people for the sum of 2s 6d (13p) each – presumably for the season – but the amount soon rose to 10s (50p). In 1904 a Mrs Penwell (no relation) was granted stall rights for the season. Photographs show the stern-looking lady, dressed from head to foot in black, dispensing bottles of lemonade to customers young and old. There is no competition in sight – she had none for several years!

It was during that first decade that many of the amenities we have today were introduced. At about the same time it was announced: 'During the summer chairs may be hired on the sands and green for one penny an hour'. That may have seemed an excessive amount because only a year later, a Mr Shenley of Hampstead, who had been granted chair rights for three years, ran into difficulties and Mr Langford, who had provided them earlier, was re-engaged. From 1909 the Council ran the beach under direct control using its own chairs (these were recorded as 75 good second-hand chairs with hoods and sundry others). Beach tents could be rented at a cost of 10s 6d (53p) for the summer. The first beach inspector was employed in 1909 at a wage of £1 a week. Both Daniel's Donkeys and Punch and Judy shows were popular with those early visitors. As late as the mid-1960s the right to offer donkey rides was granted to G. Daniels, and to Mr J.T. Stafford to present Punch and Judy shows. Many of the children who crowded around the small stand to cheer and boo the activities of Mr Punch his wife Judy and dog Toby remember the Staffords with affection. After many years with not a donkey in sight, and a century since their first appearance, Julie Wibrow has her placid creatures plying for hire on Paignton Sands.

Locals have never thronged on Corbyn Beach like its neighbour, although from 1928 it did become possible to walk under the sea wall from Torre Abbey Sands when the platform between the two was finally completed. Photographs taken in the first decade of the century show that there were private tents along the whole beach. The owners paid an annual rent to the Council for the site only. Their successors at Corbyn today are still private but the designs are more in keeping with the times.

The erosion of the soft sandstone of the district produces fine red sand and that, in turn, has resulted in 'the best beaches' being at Paignton and Goodrington.

Ralph Penwill told the story of Paignton's history through the eyes of a council official and how, early in the century, his employers had conducted beach business. He explains that, in 1899, Paignton

Fishcombe Cove, near Brixham, which had more bathers in the 1950s and 1960s than one is likely to see today. As this postcard shows, it had refreshment facilities in those days.

In 1912 a beach photographer paid the Council 2s

Shoalstone open-air pool at Brixham – a popular attraction in post-war years and still open during the summer months.

6d (13p) for a season's concession. At the same time residents erecting their own tents on the Sands were permitted to do so on a payment of 10s (50p) for the season 'as compared with £2 10s which is the inclusive cost to visitors'. At this time there were about 300 tents in a double-row north of the pier. They were, not surprisingly, very popular with Paigntonians, but were something of an eyesore to visitors. Earlier, the privately-owned Paignton Bathing Company had sold all their bathing machines to the Council (30 in all – with office and equipment – for £1,425). These were soon sold off and a bathing station put up in their place – the bathing machine era had gone forever. Its replacement remained on the Sands for many years, being hoisted in and out each season by a huge crane.

There was another innovation in 1924. The growing sport of 'surf or plank riding' was advertised: 'Planks are rapidly towed by motor boats, and the sport consists in riding the planks in standing positions by the aid of a guiding rope to ensure balance'. Modest beginnings for what is still one of our most popular seaborne activities.

Popular with the children

The fine red sands at Goodrington, washed clean by the sea twice daily, seem to have come to public notice early in the century when the Council in 1908 erected a free bathing shed but as it was constantly attacked by vandals, it was removed eight years later. There were also many complaints about young men bathing naked!

Although development was most rapid between the wars, its popularity was enhanced when some enterprising boatmen began running motor launches from Paignton to the South Sands. In 1919 a tea stall for refreshments was permitted on North Sands, the concession costing the tenant only 5s (25p) for the season. Another stall, on South Sands, followed in 1921. As land was bought over the next few years, huts and tents were provided in a somewhat haphazard fashion – but Goodrington Sands became a Mecca both for residents and holidaymakers. Goodrington Cottage, the home of the Misses Brown, was bought in 1922 with over 12 acres of garden (although the house was not demolished for over a decade). In the same year,

The old Freshwater quarry at Brixham, from which stone was taken to build the Breakwater. In this 1950s scene there is a tea hut in the foreground and a car park.

Goodrington's photographic rights were sold for the first time, the lucky photographer paying just £4 for the season. The last decade before World War Two saw the introduction of several smaller projects. These included the construction of the South Sands cabin terraces in 1932 and these remained popular for the next 50 years. The arrival of more holidaymakers after the war necessitated the urgent provision of new facilities. A children's playground was a popular innovation and in 1946 the Scootaboat fleet of 15 boats was replaced.

The cliffs on both sides of Brixham harbour means that beaches are few and far between. To the west is Churston Cove (Fishcombe is adjacent) and to the southeast St Mary's Bay. Both are accessible only via steep paths. Nearer the town centre is Breakwater Beach. For many years Breakwater Beach was a shipyard. Robert Jackman built many vessels there from the 1850s up to about 1912 when he moved his operation nearer town. During World War Two it became a shipyard again. It was used by Upham & Co during the time when it was undertaking major work for the Admiralty. Some 1,000 vessels were constructed or repaired in Brixham between 1939 and 1945.

There has been an open-air swimming pool at Shoalstone Point nearby for many years. It was last reconstructed in 1934 when a shallow end especially for children was included. In 1975 there were demands for it to be closed as the quality of the water was reportedly not up to standard. However, Shoalstone remains open despite doubts about its long-term future surfacing from time to time. An incident in 1985, which resulted in Torbay Council being required to pay huge damages, did not stop its continuing use during the summer and questions are, once more, being asked about whether the pool is safe for bathers. After minor repairs were completed, it re-opened for the summer in June 2003.

From horseless carriage to the jet

JUST over a century ago a new arrival warranted a special news item in the paper. In August 1899 it was reported that one Dr Gough was the first person in Torquay to own a motor car. Unfortunately we do not know the name of the proud owner of the second, but the third such vehicle, a single-cylinder Benz, belonged to Councillor Angell. When the 20th century dawned there were just three private cars driving around the streets of the town. The first local traffic-related death was almost a decade away.

Steam railways

With the exception of the tramways (which had a relatively short-lived life between 1907 and 1934) the other 'rail-roads' around Torbay were well established by 1900. The railway had reached Torquay as early as 1849 and the line had been continued through Livermead to Paignton in 1859 and on to the River Dart a little later. 'Mr Wolston's Little Line' ran from the rather unexpected terminus at Churston to Brixham.

Like so many other parts of the country, the Beeching cuts resulted in the Brixham branch closing in May 1963. As late as 1959 there had been 12 trains a day during the week, and 17 on Saturdays but the line was said to be losing £10,000 a year. The last train of the day left the station at the top of the hill in early evening, but Devon General buses ran into the town centre until much later in the day. The

The view from Brixham station in the early 1960s, looking down the line to Churston.

Churston station with its bay platform on the left from where trains left on the branch line to Brixham, which was closed in 1963.

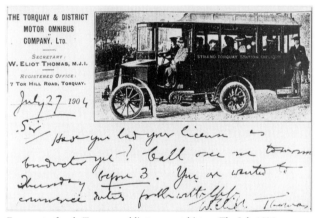

Fragment of early Torquay public transport history. The July 1904 message to a potential employee reads: 'Have you had your license (sic) as conductor yet? Call and see me tomorrow Thursday before 3. You are wanted to commence duties forthwith.' The letter was sent by W. Eliot Thomas, secretary of the Torquay and District Motor Omnibus Company Ltd, which had its office at 7 Tor Hill Road.

Early 20th-century omnibus standing in Torbay Road, Torquay, ready for its service to Paignton. This is from a postcard sent in 1904 to 'Master Glanville Turle, Abbey Mount, Torquay – Do you remember riding on this, with Grandma, to Paignton last month?' The date of the card suggests this is one of the first of the GWR buses.

line from Paignton to Kingswear suffered a similar fate but there was a rebirth when the Dart Valley Railway took control in 1972.

Steam and motor omnibuses

Perhaps surprisingly steam was used in the first public service transport road vehicles in Torbay. The man who instigated this service, Mr Adams, had experience of steam as he ran the *Princess May* ferry service from Paignton Pier. His first bus was the LIFU (it looked rather like a steam-boat on wheels). A great step forward was made in 1903 when the Torquay and District Motor Omnibus Company introduced purpose-built Clarksons into service around Torquay. They were single-deck saloons with aluminium bodies. Heating was by a paraffin burner and there were 20 litres of water under the seats. They were chain-driven, had hard tyres and 15 seats. The first service was between Chelston and the Strand through the town centre. The fare between the Clock Tower and Chelston was 2d. There were eventually eight such vehicles in the fleet and they were sold to a company in Harrogate just two months before the trams arrived. It was said the directors feared that the competition would bankrupt their business.

Another local company, formed in 1911, survived for many years. The Torquay-Chelston Steam Car

GWR buses pictured in Station Square, Paignton, in 1905.

An unidentified and undated charabanc trip about to depart from outside the Town Hall in Brixham, probably in the early 1920s. The 'No 15' on the cab door suggests this is a Grey Torpedo charabanc.

Company ran its service from Watcombe Pottery to Chelston avoiding the parts covered by the Tramway Company. During World War One it managed to keep running by employing conductresses, considered a daring move at the time. The word Steam in its title was dropped in 1922 when it acquired a Leyland motor (petrol) chassis (to which

the body of the old bus was fixed). The company was bought out by the Devon General in 1927.

On 11 July 1904 the Great Western Railway started running motor omnibuses between Torquay and Paignton. There were two motor buses, one single and one double-decker (the Licensing Committee allowed it to carry 36 passengers, 16

Reliance Cars ran charabanc trips from Torquay in the years following World War One. This one was dated July 1919 by the photographer, Vickery Brothers of Paignton.

The Burton buses in Brixham serviced local needs for excursions – these regulars at the Blue Anchor Inn in Fore Street are all set for a day trip, probably to Dartmoor. The Burton buses may have gone – but the Blue Anchor lives on.

inside, 18 on top and two beside the driver). The fare for the complete journey was 4d but there were soon complaints that 2d for short journeys was excessive. Over the next 60 years local bus services were to expand so much that the Devon General's services into Brixham contributed to that particular wielding of the Beeching Axe. Other additions made in those early days included services from Paignton

The Burton buses were once a common sight around Brixham's roads, right through to the 1980s. The company was bought by Devon General in 1988.

to Totnes and to Brixham but the latter ran only in the summer because it was considered to be taking passengers from the railway. A popular round-trip today is the bus ride to Totnes, then down the River Dart by launch to Dartmouth, by ferry to Kingswear and the short journey back to Paignton by steam train. A through-ticket is also available in the reverse direction. This is not a new idea – the whole was on offer before 1910. In those days guidebooks referred to the river trip as 'the journey down the English Rhine'.

Another company operating from both Torquay

Wartime measures for Devon General as it experiments with a gas burning engine in February 1943.

Devon General on service in Torquay – the bus for Paignton (above) is about to leave the old bus station in Palk Street, while the 1953 shot (below) shows the No 50 Ellacombe and St Marychurch service negotiating the Mallock Memorial clock tower on the Strand.

and Paignton was Grey Torpedo Cars. The word Torpedo was later dropped from the title and as Grey Cars it operated for several decades. Although the company has passed through various hands in recent years, it is still possible to travel in Grey Cars on pleasure trips around Devon. During World War One its vehicles were requisitioned for war service (London General omnibuses are often seen on television documentaries – carrying troops to battle in Flanders) but it is not known if any of the Grey Cars ever came back to Torbay. However, Italian Lancias were bought when business resumed in 1919. The GWR continued to operate from Paignton to Totnes running on coal-gas that was kept in a huge gas-envelope on the roof. Some local services were operated in this manner in the 1940s – and caused great amusement both to passengers and pedestrians.

The Devon General Bus Company came into existence in 1919 and ran in opposition to the Torquay Tramway Company (which had decided to run omnibuses as well as trams). Realising the importance of the growing port of Brixham, the former began operating a service from Hyde Road

Paignton's Station Square perhaps in the 1940s, with the Western National single-decker about to leave for Totnes. In those days, almost all cars were black.

(from the existing tramway terminus). Competition was intense, particularly on the route between Torquay and Paignton and the matter was resolved only when the Tramway Company bought out the Devon General, transferring all bus services to it. In the decade that followed there was a rapid growth in both leisure and commuter services. The opportunities to travel to work in Paignton have been well documented. In 1924 the GWR commenced a new service to Totnes using 'a fleet of cars on pneumatic tyres'. They ran from Paignton, every hour on the hour from 9am to 8pm. Other tour companies in Paignton at this period were: Comfy Cars, Redcliffe Cars and Reliance Cars (using 20-seater Lancias with 'double pneumatic tyres'). There were many other small operators at that time: Mr Mill's Bluebird service; the Paigntonian and Ashcroft's and Burton, among them. Brixham people will recall that the Burton Buses continued to run from the town centre to Kingswear well into the 1980s.

The Trams

The proposed coming of the tramways to Torquay (and later to Paignton) caused such a major upheaval that it was not surprising that the steam

bus directors took fright. After much controversy it was decided that the trams should be a private enterprise and the Torquay Tramway Company was formed in 1905. The directors' decision was not to use the more common overhead trolleys but to use the Dolter Surface Contact System instead. Self-operating studs between the rails provided the electrical power when a skate attached beneath each tram activated them. The work took 18 months to complete and the whole town was shut down street-by-street to enable the tracks and power cables to be laid. The first tram left the depot in Plainmoor in December 1906, and during early 1907 the fleet became operational. There were 18 cars, all built by Brush of Loughborough. Possible problems with the studs in the road first surfaced when, according to a newspaper report, 'Mr Hannaford, a cab proprietor, was driving his cab in Torre when it crossed the tramway and the horse stepped on to a contact-stud which by some means happened to be alive. The electric current felled the horse immediately and in a few moments it was dead'.

The Dolter system was abandoned and the extension to Paignton in 1911 was by overhead trolley – the rest of the town being converted at the same time. Trams were very popular from

Inside Devon General's depot on Newton Road, itself now only a memory. The Bayline mini-buses are pictured in 1986, their first year of operation; the flat-fronted Atlantean double-deckers were snapped 20 years previously.

Two fascinating studies of the tramlines being laid in Torquay before the service started in 1907. The group of navvies pausing from their work for the photographer are in Union Street outside the then Torbay Hospital, while the shot of them hard at work was taken on Newton Road near Torre Station.

Laying the rails for the Torquay tramways in 1906–7 must have caused immense disruption, even allowing the traffic levels in those days. These two pictures (below and next page) were taken at Torre, this one looking along Union Street towards town.

This is in the opposite direction back along Newton Road.

It must have been a great day for Torquay when the tram service came into operation in April 1907. Pictured here are the first trams lined up on Victoria Parade, with the harbour scene in the background; the other picture is from the other end of the line up and is from a postcard in which the publisher wasn't quite careful enough with his facts – he has overprinted the wrong date of 1906. The card does, however, have the advantage of some sailing ship atmosphere.

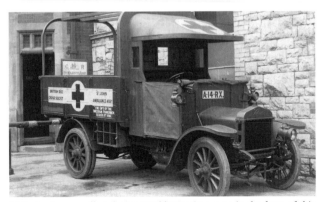

Help for the war effort during World War One came in the form of this ambulance for the Red Cross and St John Ambulance; 'The gift of the Brixham fishermen, March 11th 1916,' says the inscription on the vehicle, seen outside the Town Hall.

their instigation and, by 1929, a report stated that 'over 109 million passengers have been carried and 11,840,000 miles covered'. Road traffic generally was increasing at this time and an attempt by the Council and the Tramway Company to introduce trolley buses was described as a plot between them to convert the town to 'this cumbersome and uncertain mode of locomotion' and that it 'had been sprung on the community without warning'.

In the event the Parliamentary Bill failed at the Committee stage and the idea was abandoned.

Blackler's Dairy in Middle Street, Brixham, opted for the new form of horse power in the 1920s.

Early aviation at Paignton. A photograph signed by F.W. Raynham, who flew his Avro biplane from Paignton beach (note the pier pavilion in the background) as part of a *Daily Mail* publicity stunt in April 1914 – the newspaper was enthusiastic about the prospects of powered flight. Raynham and the French flyer, Henri Salmet (above) flew 23 flights over seven days. Salmet had flown in from Paris in this Bleriot monoplane but the machine proved unreliable and made few flights.

Within three years the trams had gone, being replaced by Devon General buses early in 1934.

Modern Times

Even today, there is little evidence that the jet age has reached Torbay except that, on a clear day, it is possible to gaze up and see the vapour trails of the high-flying aircraft winging their way in and out of the country. Their flight-plans, however, take them right over Berry Head because situated there is an electronic beacon which forms part of the air traffic control system. Technically known as a VOR Beacon, it looks from the air like a landed spaceship.

Bringing in the visitors

BRIXHAM, with its maritime connections and a prosperous fishing fleet, did not need to seek visitors on any great scale until, as we will see, the industry went into decline in the first decade of the 20th century.

A guidebook written about 1910 expresses Brixham's charms well: 'The equability of the Climate of South Devon, together with the unusual amount of sunshine which it enjoys, has raised Torquay to its position as the Queen of Watering Places. Brixham, while sharing in these genial conditions, possesses features which make it even more desirable. It is sheltered on the west side (the source of prevailing winds) by a lofty ridge of hills… In winter it is almost unknown for snow to lie for any length of time… House rents are low, apartments are cheap and the sanitary arrangements are thoroughly modern. There are three classes of people to whom Brixham should make a direct appeal: the intending resident, the invalid and the holiday maker. The invalid will find the equability of its climate and the extraordinary amount of sunshine, combined with the choice of two distinct climates, a powerful agency in the restoration of health and vigour. Brixham is particularly suitable to old people to whom the extremes of temperature

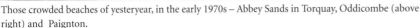
Those crowded beaches of yesteryear, in the early 1970s – Abbey Sands in Torquay, Oddicombe (above right) and Paignton.

Post-war GWR advertising poster for Brixham, emphasising the picturesque nature of the port.

Railway posters for Paignton stressed the beach aspect.

Torquay posters – the earlier example concentrates on the health giving properties of the resort, while the later one has a more cosmopolitan feel, and the use of the 'English Riviera' concept.

A Torbay tourism poster from modern days, featuring the English Riviera's 'tickling stick' palm tree logo which was at the centre of several award winning campaigns.

This was the old coach station in 1951, on land which is now the Town Hall car park in Torquay.

are trying and dangerous, patients convalescent after severe illness and sufferers from nervous diseases, over-work and malnutrition. The holidaymaker finds a country which is neither spoiled nor vulgarised'.

Paignton at first tried to remain aloof from the new tourism. Day-trippers were bringing prosperity to many South Coast towns but an early guidebook says: 'Here you will find no rollicking horse-play and boisterous fun such as you have become accustomed to [elsewhere], Paignton prefers to be select, dignified and discreet'. Later it too, like Torquay, was making a great effort to encourage visitors. Paignton stressed the wonderful sands, whilst Torquay had been encouraging invalids to seek the 'airs' for over half a century.

It is perhaps ironic that just when Brixham was offering hope to sick and ill, Torquay was seeking to change from being a select watering place to become a holiday resort for summer visitors. At the end of the century the town had become a municipal borough, with a mayor and corporation, and there was an urge to make the town more and more prosperous and progressive. In addition there had been a large increase in its boundary and population, St Marychurch and Cockington (Chelston)

In the 1960s Torquay's coach station in Lymington Road was a busy place, with holidaymakers arriving from all parts of the country.

The Shedden Hill area of Torquay in October 1952 – not a tourism picture at first sight but the scene was to change dramatically because of the visitor numbers and the growing influence of the motor car. The allotment areas on both sides of the path were soon to become a car park.

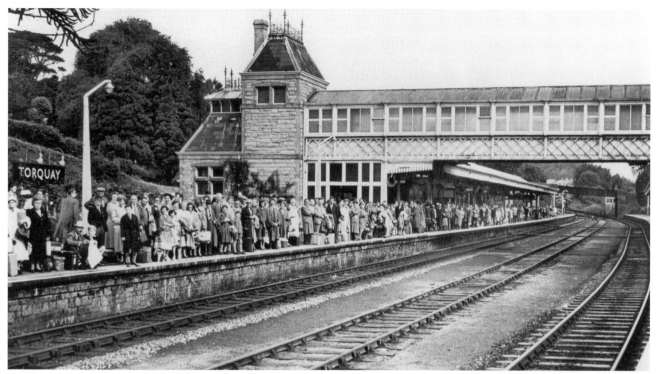

A 1960s scene at Torquay Station as the holidaymakers wait for their trains home.

Fun for the visitors in 1968, when Torbay became a new county borough formed from the councils of the Three Towns of Torquay, Paignton and Brixham.

were now part of a Torquay of 36,000 people against 26,000 just a year or so earlier. In April 1900 the Council made the decision to 'advertise Torquay in the *Morning Leader* and other newspapers'. That first modest move was to develop into the massive, and highly expensive, press and television campaigns of today. It is worth recording that picture posters were rejected and condemned as 'poor publicity'. Soon after, in 1902, an information bureau for visitors was set up. A forerunner of the Torbay Tourist Board, with its municipal links, stems from a decision made in November 1911 to set up a Borough Entertainment Committee. The Torquay Chamber of Commerce had already – in 1906 – become involved in publicity and raised £300 for the purpose. A year later there were problems raising funds – this has

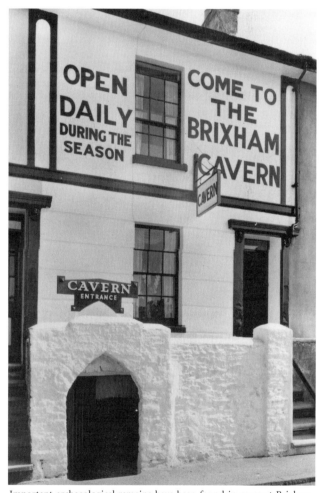

Important archaeological remains have been found in caves at Brixham, though it is many years since the Brixham Cavern (discovered in 1858) in Mount Pleasant Road was a tourist attraction. It was finally closed in 1977.

been an ongoing difficulty; a century on there are still complaints of having not enough money to do the job properly.

Sea fishing trips have long been a staple at Brixham harbour. Pictured here in the 1970s are, from the left, George Martin, George Dyer, boatowner Mr Lang, and Derek Trust.

The primitive look of the early Ayreville Holiday Camp on the Totnes road out of Paignton.

The Fort Tea House at Berry Head, Brixham, from a 1930s postcard.

The entrance to Louville Holiday Camp at Berry Head, with St Mary's Bay in the background. This card was published by Hamilton Fisher and Co, 3 Pimlico, Torquay.

Fun for the visitor – a carnival waitress race taking part in Torbay Road, Paignton, in 1966.

Holidays for all

The change of gauge from Brunel's Broad to Standard in the early 1890s resulted in through trains coming for the first time from the Midlands and the North. The popularisation of the Torbay towns as a mass holiday destination seems to have started with the 'Rochdale excursionists' a few years later in 1897. As a result of good publicity by the Rochdale Merchants and Tradesmen's Association 3,000 day-trippers arrived in six special trains, the first at 7.25, the last at 9.40am. In addition, another 2,000 came from Devonport in two special trains. The whole event was repeated two years later when 2,500 arrived in seven specials. Most were again in the town for just one day although we are told that 200 had purchased 16 one-day and 500 eight-day tickets. Longer-stay visitors were being sought in those early days. The real leap forward however, was a decade or so later during the 1913 Whitsun Bank Holiday. The *Daily News and Leader* organised a special non-stop, numbered-seat excursion from London to Torquay. Some 500 people travelled in 'ten claret-coloured corridor coaches drawn by the giant engine *King James*'. The 199-mile trip took just 207 minutes according to one enthusiast who travelled with stop-watch in hand. According to the *Torquay Directory* the passengers enjoyed separate cars for 'smoking, ladies, luncheon and tea cars, all for a modest return fare of 17s 0d' (85p).

In the last two or three years cruise liners carrying

Louville Camp, Paignton – a 1980s housing estate now occupies most of this area.

Brixham Holiday Camp.

mainly American tourists have been visiting the River Dart. Now, in the 21st century it seems that these vessels will be anchoring in Torbay also and disembarking travellers to see the sights of South Devon. Nearly 80 years ago, the 14,000-ton Cunard cruise liner *Antonia* brought between 500 and 600 holidaymakers to the town. This must have been a boost to the local economy, needed then as it was during the Great Depression of the 1930s. One statistic from 1938 is of particular interest. Over the August Bank Holiday weekend 20,000 people arrived in Torquay, and 50 additional excursion trains came in on the Sunday from London, Wales, Bristol and the Midlands. Fares at that time were competitive. A cheap day ticket to Plymouth from Torquay cost 3s 2d (16p); a trip to the Empire Exhibition in Glasgow just 30s 3d (a little over £1.50p).

The lounge bar at the Devon Coast and Country Club, on the Paignton ring road where new housing now stands.

Dolphin Holiday Camp at Brixham.

Dining hall at the South Devon Holiday Camp on the ring road at Paignton. Today's visitors would require something a little more sophisticated.

Enjoying the fresh air at St Mary's Bay Holiday Camp, Brixham.

Earlier, Torbay had seen the start of the holidays-by-coach era – although the numbers must have been small compared with the number of visiting coaches seen around our streets today. In June 1932 some 250 visitors were staying in Torquay having come from the cotton mills at Nelson, Lancashire on a special charabanc tour. It was not only the large hotels that profited, but also small hotels and boarding houses.

The outbreak of World War Two reduced the number of holidaymakers to almost nil but some 50,000 aircrew trained in Torbay between 1940 and 1943. Many of the survivors returned with their families and this boosted the numbers of visitors in the immediate post-war years. The first peacetime summer, in 1946, brought 20,000 visitors for the August Bank Holiday weekend. There were still problems with food shortages. Just a few days earlier bread rationing had started.

The rise of the overseas holiday and the decline of holidays at home meant that Torbay had to be marketed like any other commodity. The Torbay Tourist Board was set up in April 1981. This is now the English Riviera Tourist Board and, for a time, great

success was reported in facts and figures as some 9,056,000 'visitor nights' used some 54,800 bed spaces.

A Marketing and Tourism division was set up when Torbay's Directorate of Strategic Services was created in 1998. Among other innovations by the division was a controversial Torbay poster, photographed in Rhodes in 1998 and which upset many locals, a revamped *Holiday Guide* (2000) and a *Riviera 2000* video. Currently efforts are being made to bring more visitors into Torbay between April and June and from September to November. The Division also maintains the Council's website.

Holiday camps had modest beginnings in Torbay. The first was The Nest in Paignton in 1925, but expansion took place in the open fields around the town in the early 1930s at Waterside, Marldon and Foxhole. A decade later Louville Camp in Dartmouth Road, owned by Miss Louisa Caunter, had opened (this is now a housing development with the same name). Miss Caunter also bought also some open fields at Berry Head, Brixham where she opened a camp with a similar name. She told her friends proudly that she had 'literally built it herself, buying in the necessary materials'.

Dixon's Luxury Holiday Camp at Paignton, probably in the 1930s. The foreground is now Smallcombe Road on the Foxhole estate, with the ring road away to the left. The small bungalows on the distant hillside in the Dunstone Park area can still be identified today.

After closure during World War Two all were opened up again in 1945, and continued to welcome campers for many years. Most, like Louville, have now closed and residential properties fill the land. However, the former Grange Court Holiday Centre, now Holbourne Torbay, remains open. Recently it was said to cover 64 acres and had 500 holiday homes on the site.

Brixham owes a great debt to the Pontin family. They ran Wall Park Camp and the Dolphin Camp

Torbay Holiday Chalets at Brixham, near Fishcombe Cove.

Early views of Paignton Holiday Camp, the first in the town and originally known as The Rest. It occupied a triangle of land fronting Kings Ash Road between Foxhole Road and Colley End Road. This general view from the hillside across Kings Ash Road shows both these roads in the days before housing dominated the scene – Foxhole Road is on the left and Colley End on the right; the camp area is now the flats at Two Acre Close.

(now derelict), from the late 1930s onwards. A similar debt is owed to Mr Leslie Boyce. When he applied for permission to develop the open fields around St Mary's Bay as a holiday camp, he leased the land between Sharkham and St Mary's Beach to Brixham Council for an acknowledged rental of £1. The land above the beach (also included) is now part of the South West Coast Path. Landscove Camp (now Landscove Holiday Village) was opened in 1929 by Mollie Currie and her mother. In that year there were just two caravans and some wooden huts. Later, 12 wooden huts and 18 converted ex-Devon General buses were bought. South Bay Holiday Park continues to prosper in the changed social and economic climate; it is now owned by John Fowler Holidays.

Caravans at Sharkham Point, Brixham, from a mid-1950s postcard with the message: 'The caravan is excellent and in a wonderful position overlooking the ocean'.

All at sea

Yachts and Yachtsmen – and 'the Big Js'

THE first major event which brought yachts of all sizes to the Bay was the Centenary Regatta in 1913. When the event resumed after World War One, *Britannia* (described as being owned by King George V and skippered by Captain Carter) raced in Torbay, first in the gaff-type rig category but the yacht was later converted to Bermuda rig with a new mast 165ft tall).

In June 1914 Shamrock IV, owned by Sir Thomas Lipton, arrived in Torbay. Trials were due to take place there for the Americas Cup race between *Shamrock III* and *Shamrock IV* (the newer yacht). Not surprisingly *Shamrock IV* won all three races. A special ornate cup was presented by the town to Sir

Thomas as a souvenir. *Shamrock IV* berthed again in Torquay in mid-July 1939 on her way across the Atlantic to take part in the race. The outbreak of World War Two, however, prevented the race from taking place. Despite five attempts at capturing the Americas Cup between 1899 and 1930, Sir Thomas, in his Shamrock yachts, was never successful.

The rise of the motor speedboat for racing began as long ago as 1924. On 19 September that year the Duke of York (later King George VI) was on an unofficial visit to Torbay during the International Motor Boat Regatta where contestants were racing for the Duke of York's trophy. Competitors came from Britain and overseas. The Duke fired the starting gun and provided a trophy. These early craft were very different from the huge monsters that take part in the Cowes-Torbay Race today.

The mid-1930s saw the last days of the great

J-class yachts competing in the Torbay Regatta in 1930 – the four yachts on the right of the picture are thought to be (from right) the Royal Yacht *Britannia* (owned by King George V), *Lulworth*, *Westward* and *White Heather*. For a further note about *Britannia* (see page 136).

When the Yachting Olympics were staged in Tor Bay in 1948 there was an official welcome to competitors at Torre Abbey by Sigfrid Edstrom, president of the Olympics Committee. The mayor of the day was Ald Denys Gilley and a crowd estimated at 10,000 watched from the adjoining meadows. The choir, seen in the picture right, was conducted by Ernest Goss and sang Roger Quilter's Non Nobis Domino. The opening ceremony took place on Monday 2 August and the closing ceremony on Friday 13 August.

'gentlemen-yachtsmen'. Yachts of all sizes would gather at Torquay; the steam yachts of the famous being anchored in the Outer Harbour beside the tall masts of the racers. One was the *Sunbeam II*, 'a

magnificent three-master of 685 tons', owned by Lord Runciman. The J-Class yachts attracted enthusiastic crowds from all over the county. In 1932 they appeared in the newspaper headlines as

Competitors from 25 countries marched past the front of Torre Abbey in their national contingents. The yachting events in the 1948 Olympics followed the main events at Wembley.

In the autumn of 2002 Torbay secured a major sailing coup by hosting the stopover after the first leg of the Around Alone race, which had started from New York. The only woman competitor, Emma Richards, is seen sailing her 60ft *Pindar* in the bay, while the aerial view shows the yachts setting off from Tor Bay on the second leg to Capetown; *Hexagon*, sailed by Graham Dalton, leads the way.

A fine aerial view of Torquay in 1968, showing how the harbour looked in pre-marina days.

'The Big Five'. These were: *White Heather*, *Britannia* (scuttled after the death of George V); *Valsheda* (still afloat today and much as she was then); *Shamrock* and *Astra* (once owned by Sir Mortimer Singer and later by H.F. Paul). Soon after *Candida* and *Endeavour* (owned by Mr T.O.M. Sopwith), were attending all Torbay's Regattas. Like Sir Thomas Lipton's attempts earlier, Sopwith's challenge for the Americas Cup in 1934 was unsuccessful. His *Endeavour II* failed again in 1937. Both these wonderful craft sailed regularly in the 1930s Torbay Regattas. The famous US yacht *Yankee*, also an Americas Cup contender, was also in Torbay. The big yachts last raced in 1936. In July 1937 the International Coronation Regatta brought many smaller classes in to Torbay, 12-metre yachts taking the place of the larger boats.

Like all other maritime activities, the Regatta did not take place between 1939 and 1945. One early decision taken after World War Two was that the yachting events of the 1948 London Olympic Games should take place on courses set out in Torbay.

Although Torquay was still recovering economically (and from bomb damage around the town), a major effort was made by the townspeople to make the event a success. A large water-tank (not dissimilar to the wartime static water reservoirs) was built on Beacon Quay. All the yachts taking part were subject to precise measurement for size and displacement. The opening ceremony took place in front of Torre Abbey, the Olympic flame being brought by relays of runners from the stadium in London. It burned outside throughout the Games. Headquarters was in the Marine Spa (now demolished) where competitors from the 25 nations taking part gathered. Olympic classes in that year were: six-metres; Stars; Dragons; Swallows and Fireflies. Stewart Morris and David Bond in Swallow Class won Britain's only yachting gold medal that year. For several decades Torbay continued to host international and other yachting events. Recently however, the lack of a good launching area has meant that some annual gatherings and championships have relocated elsewhere. The

Before Torquay Marina could be built, Haldon Pier had to be extended to give more protection from bad weather. A huge concrete caisson was constructed in the harbour and floated into position, as shown by this picture dating from June 1984. Below: Also in 1984, few signs yet of the marina in this picture of a corner of the harbour close to the Princess Theatre – if one stands at this point now the view out of the harbour entrance is blocked by the pier extension mentioned above.

February 1988 and there is little left of Upham's shipyard at Brixham – by June 1989 the Prince William Quay development of up-market apartments was well under way.

situation is unlikely to change in the foreseeable future.

In the autumn of 2002 the Around Alone yacht race made Torbay its only European port of call. It was the first time in its history that there had been a European stop-over. The vessels left Newport, Rhode Island in mid-September. The race restarted from Torbay in October. Brixham housed the race village. This race for solo-yachtsmen is the longest in the world and is owned by Clipper Ventures (which is chaired by Sir Robin Knox-Johnston). Major sponsors included the *Herald Express*, among others.

Yacht Marinas

About two decades ago a new word appeared in Torbay together with a new concept. The marina offered a safe anchorage, moorings and, in

A fish market worker hoses down the fish at Brixham's old fish market, which operated in full view of the public.

Brixham's new fish quay and market nears completion in October 1970.

some places, luxury living accommodation for yacht-owners and sailing enthusiasts. Torquay Marina was completed in 1984 and the former Pavilion refurbished as part of the project. No residential flats could be built on the restricted site, but there was, and still is, a secure underground car park for boat-owners and users of the facilities. The *Herald Express* told the full story thus: 'It was widely known by harbour users that the harbour was particularly vulnerable when south-east gales were blowing [and so] a stipulation was made that an extension to the Haldon pier must be carried out before a marina could be constructed. A 1/125th scale model was made by the Hydraulics Research Laboratory and tests carried out under varying wind and wave conditions. In order to ensure satisfactory conditions the Pier would have to be extended by 40 metres (120 feet). The developers decided to achieve this by constructing a huge reinforced concrete caisson (120 x 40 feet and 35 feet high) which contained 2,700 tons of concrete and 300 tons of sand. This was constructed in the harbour, towed and sunk in position and then filled with 7,300 tons of gravel'. Looking at the harbour wall today, there is no visible 'join' and the extension looks just like the original pier that was built nearly a century and a half ago.

At Brixham a more ambitious scheme was envisaged by the American Charles B. Fleming and his associates. He promised a marina, 64 residential units, club-house and ample parking. Fleming encountered financial problems and it was not until 1990 that Marina Developments took over. By the summer of 1991 the promenade between the harbour and the breakwater was completed, the first shops and a restaurant opened. Some of the flats had been occupied but the complex, built by Midas, was not completed until the late 1990s. The spectacular views across the Bay are now further enhanced by the mooring in the marina below of the Trinity Sailing Foundation's classic sailing trawlers including *Vigilance*, *Pilgrim*, *Golden Vanity*, *Leader* and *Regard* (built originally as *Our Boy* by Uphams). *Provident* came from Salcombe to join the Brixham boats.

A Rich Harvest from the Sea – the Brixham fishing industry

Catching fish for food dates back to medieval times and possibly before. The monks at Torre Abbey had permission to fish in Torbay but that most likely was for their own table. The real 'leap-forward', however, took place in the late 18th century with the

Filleting fish in the new fish market in the 1970s. Pictured are Malcolm Ansell, left, and Albert Jansen, who had been a refugee from Belgium during World War Two.

development of trawl fishing. The Brixham men probably witnessed their Continental colleagues using this method and brought the technique back home. By the start of the 20th century there were Brixham families settled around the South Coast and eastward as far as Great Yarmouth, in Wales at Tenby and Milford Haven, and in the fishing villages of southern Ireland.

The first steam-trawler, *Bertha*, was built experimentally in Dartmouth in 1870 to the designs of George Parker Bidder, the Devon-born 'calculating boy' – mathematics prodigy who had grown up to become a talented engineer. The new boat was brought around Berry Head to fish out of Brixham but the venture was not successful. Local owners, however, continued to have complete faith in sail. One old salt was bitterly critical. Speaking to a newspaper reporter he said: 'No, sir, they cost too much to work. There was a steam trawler here but she hadn't the power to

get about. Our smacks would beat her hollow any time!' Eventually the battle was lost, but it took some time. By 1900 there were several hundred steam-vessels working out of the East Coast ports but Brixham still had a fleet of 250 sailing trawlers, of which 135 were of the largest class. As well as fishing, Brixham had other industries that employed many men and provided employment for those who did

To enable residents and visitors to see trawlers at the new fish quays an elevated viewing platform was built at Brixham harbour. This picture is from 1993.

The crew of the *Provident*, with skipper William Pillar second right. From a postcard published by the Paignton photographer J.H. Germon and Sons, inscribed 'Capt W Pillar and crew, Brixham Heroes'.

not go to sea. There were the ropewalks or roperies (where ropes of all sizes were made) and sail-makers. Most of the ropewalks closed down during World War One.

Those tan-coloured sails that made the Brixham trawler different from all others were the result of treatment in the barking sheds. The bark came from oak trees and, we are told, was designed to make the canvas more durable, prevent mildew, etc. The other ingredients were Stockholm tar, tallow, red and yellow ochre. Each skipper had his own proportions for the mix (which resulted in every tan colour being different).

Although many fishermen were called up for the Royal Navy during World War One, the population still had to be fed and the boats continued to go out in all weathers. There was an additional hazard. In December 1916 a large U-boat attacked the fishing boats in the Channel. Six smacks were sunk in one week. One Brixham boat and her crew achieved fame in that war. On 31 December 1914 the Fifth Battle Squadron, with *HMS Nelson* as flagship, was in the Channel about 12 miles south east of Berry Head, prior to a gunnery practice. At 02.00 on New

Year's Day 1915 *HMS Formidable*, the last and eighth in line, was struck by a German torpedo. A sudden storm blew up and the winds reached gale-force and the sea became mountainous. Many of the rafts and boats containing survivors were swamped and overturned. It was during the rescue operation that the Brixham trawler *Provident* arrived on the scene and, through skillful seamanship by the three crew, pulled some 70 men from the sea. In spite of this, and other rescuers' efforts, some 600 Naval seamen perished that day. The fishermen all received cash rewards from Winston Churchill and were given silver medals for saving life at sea.

Those fishermen who survived the war returned to find their boats and equipment out-of-date and the fleet less than 90 in number. The new fishing grounds on the East Coast were nearer the large city markets. For some Brixham men there was the opportunity to take employment with the wealthy yacht-owners who paid excellent wages to experienced seamen. In 1935 there were just 25 boats going to sea; three years later only half-a-dozen. The once-famous fleet was almost extinct.

Rebuilding the industry after 1945 was even

In later years a second *Provident* was used as a racing vessel and is seen here, right, competing in the Channel in the Torbay-Lisbon race in 1957. The ship on the left was the *Flying Clipper*, from Sweden.

more difficult and it was another 20 years later when a fishing co-operative was set up that things began to improve. This was successful immediately and, in 1971, the new fish quay, market building, ice-plant, slipway and offices were completed. This met the trawler-men's requirements for the next decade. When additional berthing and landing facilities were opened in February 1991 it was said that about £4.6 million had been spent on improvements in the last 20 years and that the industry was then 'worth £30 million per annum'. By the mid-1990s the scrapping of vessels was very

much on the agenda and Brixham fishermen were told that millions of Euro-money was available. In May 2000 it was announced that the EU was looking for a Europe-wide reduction in fish catches and more local boats would have to be scrapped. Matters had become even more desperate by mid-2002. Further reductions in the fleet seemed certain and government ministers visited Torbay to explain the changes coming into force on 1 January 2003. The problem of crews throwing back over-quota fish into the sea is unlikely to be resolved quickly.

In the Navy

The Fleet's in port again

FOR nearly 100 years after Trafalgar, the Royal Navy ruled the waves and there were no conflicts requiring its services. Problems in the colonies in Africa, India and elsewhere had been Army matters but it was during the first decade of the 20th century that the first signs of a new enemy nearer home were becoming visible. The German Kaiser, Wilhelm II, was expanding his navy in furtherance of his ambitious plans to increase international trade and, thus, his country's influence overseas; in five years up to 1902 the Germans used their technological skills to become a major naval power.

A bigger navy

By 1905 Britain had begun a concerted effort to catch up with her German cousins. In July 113 ships were anchored in Tor Bay – described at the time as 'the largest assemblage ever'. Two years earlier a visit of the Home Fleet had caused no Press notice. To meet the mounting German challenge the Navy ordered the construction of *HMS Dreadnought*. Up to this time all battleships carried four big guns and many smaller ones. *Dreadnought* was the first to have ten 12in guns and with a speed of over 20 knots could outrun any other battleship in the world. So impressive were her armaments that her name was given to an entire class of vessels and came into

Looking over Princess Pier to where the Royal Navy made a fine sight, anchored in Tor Bay for a royal fleet review in 1910.

The Royal Yacht *Victoria and Albert* moves through the fleet in Tor Bay in 1910.

A souvenir postcard of the 1910 review, with the caption: 'Combined fleets of British warships in Tor Bay July 1910. The Dreadnoughts'.

popular use to describe all heavily-armed battleships. She made her first appearance when the Channel Fleet was anchored in the Bay from the 9–14 May 1907.

Mr White, aviator

It was just three years later that a modest aviator was to make a flight over the British Fleet that was to change the course of naval history. The new king and his wife, George V and Queen Mary, were on board the Royal Yacht *Victoria and Albert* to review the Fleet in Mount's Bay, Cornwall, when stormy weather there necessitated its transfer at a day's

Pioneer aviator Claude Grahame-White flies over the fleet in 1910, having taken off from Torre Abbey meadows.

The fleet was in port again during 1924 when this postcard was published. Note the smoke from the Marine Spa boiler house chimney.

The Royal Yacht *Britannia* pictured in Torbay in July 1969, pursued by a flotilla of small boats after having moved through the Western Fleet.

to demonstrate to the Admiral of the Fleet, the King, the utility of the flying-machine in the naval warfare of the future.' When the forced transfer took place Grahame-White first announced his intention of flying from Cornwall to Torquay, he eventually travelled with his plane to Newton Abbot by train and instead of coming the last six miles by air the Farman biplane was brought by road into a field (now the Abbey Gardens) 'at the bottom of Belgrave Road fronting the Belgrave Hotel, to remain under police protection so that it would be ready for a flight over the war-vessels in the bay'. At first light the ships were enveloped in a thick haze and so the success of any flight was doubtful. However, the weather improved at about midday and we are told that the sun shone fitfully. Shortly after one o'clock White 'ascended his seat' and his mechanic started the seven-cylinder Gnome engine, and he commenced his take-off uphill rising in the air 'like a horse at a fence and was up and over the Royal Yacht in a flash'. Once in the air Grahame-White made two flights over

notice to Torbay. The *Torquay Directory* told the story of the day's events: 'Mr White, the owner of a fragile wood-and-canvas aeroplane, was determined the Fleet, the first in the early afternoon when he 'exhibited the possibilities of the aeroplane in attack; the second in the evening when he showed its use for

Claude Grahame-White pictured at Torquay.

Preparing to get Grahame-White's aircraft off the ground in Torre Abbey meadows.

Moment of take-off in 1910, which naturally attracted the inquisitive crowds. The centre carriage was that of the Grant family, of Grant's marble works in Teignmouth Road. The carriage is said to have contained William Henry Godfrey Grant and his wife Emma, and their sons Godfrey, aged 11, and Harry, 19. Young Godfrey is said to have had a flight with White, at a cost of 7s 6d (37p).

defence against invading warships'. On this occasion he reached the height of some 500 metres. The *Daily Mail* told its readers the following morning how Grahame-White had given the King and Queen 'an unforgettable thrill which comes with the first sight of the miracle of an aeroplane in flight'. The paper concluded: 'The heavy broadsides of the super-Dreadnoughts were helpless and ineffective against him. Not a single gun could be elevated to an angle that could reach him. Laden with a supposed cargo

The Royal Navy frigate *HMS Torquay* was adopted by the town in 1960 and a contingent from the ship is pictured here marching to the Town Hall to be entertained by the Mayor in February 1961. South-east gales wrecked much of the visit but the sailors did visit Plainmoor, and saw Hull City beat Torquay United 2-1.

active service unit in Torquay late in that war. It has been suggested that the creation of the Royal Naval Air Service in 1914 was, in part at least, the result of Grahame-White's pioneering flight over the Fleet in 1910. Towards the end of hostilities the Royal Air Force was providing air cover from Torquay Harbour using Short 184 seaplanes. Officially the Marine Operations (Seaplane and Balloon) Station, it had 12 aircraft engaged on anti-submarine duties in the Channel. These were kept in the Coastlines shed which had been specially converted for them, and other buildings erected on Beacon Quay. They took off and landed in the sea off Haldon Pier. A large crane erected there lifted them in and out of the water. This all happened just after the Royal Naval Air Service and the Royal Flying Corps merged in April 1918 to become the RAF. Beacon Quay was the base for 239 squadron, RAF. This squadron remained in the town until May 1919. Earlier, in July 1918, the RAF, taking advantage of the Defence of the Realm Act, had acquired land compulsorily at the Old Fort on Berry Head to establish a kite observation balloon station. Little is

of the as-yet uninvented X-power explosive that the advent of the aeroplane renders inevitable, he had £100,000,000 worth of the British Navy helpless beneath him, caught in the narrow waters of the enclosed bay'. It was only little over 30 years later that the Japanese were using air power at Pearl Harbor to destroy a great United States battle fleet enclosed in the narrow waters of an enclosed bay.

Most of the action in the World War One was in theatres far removed from Torbay, but there was one

Early submarines in Torquay harbour in 1915, from a postcard dated that year.

One of the submarines entering Torquay harbour in 1915.

known about this operation. In December 1918, when the captured U161 arrived, 'water-planes flew in the air, descended on to the water' much to the enjoyment of the crowds who assembled on the Pier.

In 1924 a large fleet of about 80 vessels were anchored in Torbay. Less than two decades later many of those battleships were lost in World War Two. Among them were *Barham, Royal Oak* and *Warspite.*

The part played by Torbay in the liberation of Europe was of great significance. It was at the end of May 1944 that the largest fleet of vessels (said to be well over 400 in number) gathered here briefly before sailing off to join the vast fleet that landed on the shores of Normandy on 6 June. Presumably because of the secrecy of Operation Overlord, there appear to be no photographs of that momentous day in history.

The most recent great gathering of British

A Torquay contingent of sailors from the Cressy class cruiser *HMS Hogue*, pictured outside the Exeter Hotel in Union Street (where Woolworths now stands) in 1912. The happiness shown here was to turn to tragedy, for the *Hogue* was sunk less than two years later and a good proportion of these lads would have lost their young lives. The ship was torpedoed by a German submarine while trying to defend the Belgian seaports at the beginning of World War One. Around half the 700 crew were lost.

warships, almost certainly the last ever, took place in July 1969 when Queen Elizabeth II, with the Duke of Edinburgh, reviewed the Western Fleet of some 40 warships off Daddyhole Plain. Thousands lined the shores of Torbay to watch.

Trips around the Bay – and beyond

AFTER the building of the Princess Pier in the 1890s pleasure boats sailed from the wooden jetty there. When the *King Edward* and the *Ethel* started a ferry service to Paignton and Brixham at about the same time, an early timetable shows that both ran from Haldon and Princess Piers. The small pier by the Pavilion (so prominent in many publicity photographs) was built by the Council for small vessels like these and was first used by them in August 1906.

The arrival of the new *Duke of Devonshire*, a large vessel designed to carry 300 passengers at a speed of over 12 knots, caused great excitement among Torquay's residents and visitors. The popularity of trips afloat resulted in the arrival two years later, in 1896, of the *Duke's* sister ship, the *Duchess of Devonshire*. Together they worked the coast for over 30 years. During the summer of 1936 the *Duke* was described as 'Your Favourite Steamer'. Sailings in mid-August were advertised widely in local newspapers: 'View the start of J-Class races; leave 10.30am, return 12.30pm. Fare 2s (10p)'. The following day there was a 'Cheap Day Trip to Sidmouth and Lyme Regis'. The cost was 3s (15p) to Sidmouth and 4s (20p) 'all the way'. Return by 10pm was promised. The *Duchess* ended her days on Sidmouth beach in 1934 landing passengers by means of a sloping ramp at the bow. Assault craft in World War Two landed troops in much the same way.

Day trips to the Channel Islands were popular from the 1930s to the 1990s. The GWR's Weymouth-based *St Patrick*, *St Julien* and *St Hellier*

A paddle steamer serving Oddicombe beach around 1910. This might well be the *Duke of Devonshire*, sister ship to the *Duchess of Devonshire*, pictured in the fine study below.

sailed to the Islands every fortnight. The fare to Guernsey was 12s 6d (63p), the trippers having five hours ashore. It was more expensive on the longer Jersey voyage, 14s 6d (73p). When *St Julien* arrived back from Guernsey in August 1938 and was unable to dock because of a thick fog, there were 870 passengers on board. These all ceased during World War Two but resumed afterwards with British Rail vessels (the GWR had been nationalised in 1948). These were finally withdrawn in 1963.

Larger vessels than those operating earlier sailed from Torquay harbour in the immediate post-war

The Torquay harbour jetty built by the council in 1906, close to Princess Gardens and the Pavilion, was a popular pleasure boat departure point.

The *Kiloran* (and later the *Kiloran 2*) will be remembered by older Torbay residents and visitors, making trips from Haldon Pier from 1947.

years. The first was the *Pride of Devon* working between 1946 and 1948. The *Lady Enchantress* was the next to arrive in 1950; she sailed from Haldon Pier. Her engines were said to be worn-out and they broke down frequently. She achieved some notoriety, first by slicing a smaller vessel in half off Brixham and then, in 1952, when on passage to Guernsey with a load of passengers, breaking down in mid-Channel. Taken in tow by the tug *Turmoil*, she ended her days in Falmouth, being broken up soon afterwards.

Another pleasure vessel still remembered by many was the *Princess Elizabeth* (371 tons and 195 feet long). Her docking was greeted with acclamation – people flocked to Haldon pier to view the new arrival. The *Princess* had been built in 1927 (the year after the birth of her namesake, the later

The *Lisieux* pictured in 1965, the year she arrived in Torbay.

Elizabeth II) and carried passengers between Southampton and Cowes for many years until 1959. In June 1940 she made two trips to the beaches at Dunkirk, rescuing 1,673 men. Her stay at Torquay, however, caused much controversy, and the Council finally withdrew fuelling facilities in September 1961. Her stay had lasted just two years.

The *SS Pioneer* leaves Brixham in the days when there was still plenty of sail in the harbour.

The *Princess Elizabeth*, a Dunkirk veteran, gave trips in the bay between 1959 and 1961. Operated by Torbay Steamers at 4 Beacon Quay, she was 198 feet long and had been built at Southampton in 1927.

The next arrival was the French Lines ship *Lisieux* in 1965, then two years later the Jersey Lines *La Duchesse de Bretagne* (formerly the BR ship *Brighton*) ran a regular service to Jersey. It carried over 80,000 passengers and 1,500 cars during the summer of 1967, and promised that the target for the next year would be '100,000 passengers and 4,000 cars'. Unfortunately the ambitious 1968 plan failed to get started. The next vessel to berth at Haldon Pier was the Penzance-Scillies vessel *Queen of the Isles* in 1970. The *Queen* ran briefly to Guernsey. A customs shed was built on Beacon Quay at this time but was never used fully.

From 1964 until 1969 the Devon Cruising Company operated the *Bateau Morgat* from

Torquay. In that year she was sold to the Dame of Sark (and became Sark's link with Guernsey). What seemed at the time to be a real acquisition to the holiday trade was the *Devon Princess II*, a £150,000 purpose-built vessel. Comedian Russ Abbott performed the naming ceremony at the Pier in 1981. This vessel operated for a short time only.

Torbay Seaways, a local company, made serious attempts to bring a Channel Isles service back to Torquay in the early 1990s, using a succession of ships: *Devoniun* (the former *Scillonian*): *Star Capricorn*, a hydrofoil (not a success) and the *Devoniun II*, formerly the McBrayne ferry, *Hebrides* – a vessel of 1,400 tons). Finally, in August 1995,

The *Regency Belle*, built in New York in 1942, in Torquay harbour.

The *Torbay Prince* in Tor Bay.

The Brixham-built *Trevarno* leaves its home harbour on a trip; below is a handbill advertising the vessel.

Condor Ferries brought its *Condor 9*, a 49-metre long catamaran that started making voyages to Guernsey and Jersey on alternate days (fare £18). It ceased operations after only two years and it seems unlikely that any similar service will be introduced in the near future.

Many older people will recall the names of the smaller vessels which took them to sea from the Haldon and Princess Piers. Very popular for only a brief time was *Trevarno*, built by Uphams in 1936. The elegant pleasure craft was requisitioned less than three years later by the Admiralty.

Many people remember the name *Kiloran* with affection. There were in fact two pleasure vessels of

The *Western Lady* ferries remain to this day an enduring sight in Tor Bay.

The first *Devoniun*, formerly the *Scillonian*, at Torquay harbour for the cross-Channel run.

THE TWIN-SCREW PASSENGER VESSEL

TREVARNO

Board of Trade Licence for
134 Passengers

The Captain is a Trinity House Pilot

TEAS AND COFFEE SERVED
2 FULLY LICENSED BARS

SAILING FROM

PRINCESS PIER DAILY

LEAVE	DUE BACK
10.45 a.m.	12.15 p.m.
2.30 p.m.	6.15 ,,
7.55 ,,	9.15 ,,

OUR SPECIAL TRIP
is to the
Beautiful River Dart

BOOKING OFFICE:
PRINCESS PIER

that name and both worked from Haldon Pier for most of their time in Torquay. Devon Cruising Company ran the first *Kiloran* from 1947. She was formerly the private yacht of Lord Strathcona (later being sold to a Greek ship owner who had her refitted in Amsterdam to become a luxury yacht). *Kiloran II* was a wartime Fairmile B-Class motor-launch, originally MGB No 583. Trips aboard her cost between 3s 9d (less than 20p) and 8s (40p).

A Southampton-owned hovercraft returns to Torquay harbour in June 1969 after a trial trip for the Works Committee. Members decided in favour of the owners operating 20-minute trips for 63 passengers at 10s (50p) each.

The Western Ladies

The fleet is now smaller than it was. The remaining vessels completed 50 years of continuous operation in 1996. It had all started in 1946 when the Edhouse family of Brixham bought four ex-naval Fairmile B-Class wooden motor launches. These were converted at Brixham and the ferry service between Brixham and Torquay began.

In 1963 the company was bought by Dawn and John Perrett. Their *Western Lady* ferry service still carries many holidaymakers, and a few commuters, across Torbay throughout the summer months.

Indoor entertainment for everybody

Enjoying classical music

EARLY in the 20th century there was demand for a new place of entertainment. Classical music clearly appealed both to residents in and visitors to Edwardian Torquay. There was then a well-established concert season. The opening event of the winter at the Bath Saloons in October 1909 was a visit by the Beecham Orchestra. The young Thomas Beecham founded his first orchestra in 1906 but this one, established that year, was 'more identified with his own personality and policy'. Paderewski gave several recitals in the 1890s and, in the first decade of the 20th, Kubelik, the 'wizard of the violin' also appeared. Later the auditorium was crowded to hear Herr Fritz Kreisler, the famous

Torquay Municipal Orchestra in the Pavilion with its long-time musical director and conductor, Ernest Goss.

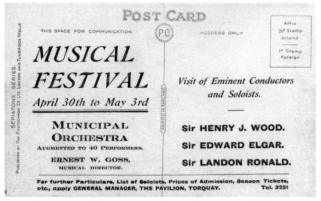

As can be seen from this promotional postcard, Ernest Goss's first Torquay Musical Festival in 1930 boasted the biggest names of the day.

Austrian violinist, open the winter concert season on 12 October 1911. In November 1912, Paderewski was back at the Bath Saloons where his recital included works by Beethoven and Chopin.

Building the Pavilion

The need for larger premises, in which all forms of entertainment could take place, was thought to be urgent. Public opinion was also pressing for the construction of 'a resort for winter visitors'. Torquay had just lost its Winter Garden, sold to Great Yarmouth for £1,300 (where it is still in use as part of the Wellington Pier complex). In addition, the small size of the Bath Saloons was not thought adequate to meet the needs of the growing borough. It took over a decade for the plan to be completed. Spa pavilions were places associated with hospitals or health resorts and this is certainly why the word 'pavilion' was chosen by the Corporation. In 1901 it was resolved 'to construct a building as near the Strand as possible'. A major step forward was made in 1903 with the final go-ahead – but that was only after a skeleton framework had been erected on the reclaimed land near Cary Green. A long debate took place as to whether it should be public-funded or a lease given to private-enterprise. In 1910 the councillors agreed that it should be a municipal enterprise. Having obtained loan sanction from the government, Mr Narracott's tender of £16,942 4s 4d was accepted. That decision had taken nearly ten years to reach. During construction it was decided to

Following the decline of music and theatre at the Pavilion, ice-skating took over before the building was redeveloped as a shopping centre. This picture is from 1979.

replace the lead of the roof with copper. The result was a building that is little changed externally today. The completed Pavilion was opened officially in 1912.

The Torquay Municipal Orchestra at work

On the day of the opening performance there was intense local enthusiasm and the first concert took place in near chaos. As early as 6pm crowds began to

Worshipping the sun in Princess Gardens in the summer of 1960, with the Princess Theatre taking shape in the background.

The coming of the Princess Theatre in 1961 brought a host of top stars to Torquay. Pictured here are Max Bygraves with a group of dancers outside the theatre in 1967, and Frankie Vaughan opening the Torquay Co-operative Society's new store in 1965.

assemble outside the pay-box and 'it was not possible to open the doors until 7.30 had been reached. At once there was a great pushing from the rear of the crowd and considerable shouting and uproar prevailed. Women screamed, some cried, and others almost fainted, so great was the crush. The first to be admitted, excited and perturbed, ran for seats and within a couple of minutes it was standing room only for the remainder'. Glass-topped tables and wicker chairs were overturned and damaged.

The first concert was by the recently formed Torquay Municipal Orchestra under the baton of Basil Hindenberg. Hindenberg had been appointed in May 1912 following the resignation of Stroud Hoxton. The first music performed was Weber's overture to *Oberon*. Prices at the first performance were: Grand Hall and Circle (numbered and reserved) 2s (10p) and 1s (5p); unreserved 6d (less than 3p). The Council appointed Mr A.M. Wilshere as its first manager. One of his early tasks had been to appoint an orchestra at a cost of £86 a week. Sir Henry Wood, then conductor of the Queen's Hall Orchestra, visited the Pavilion in July 1914. Delighted with the performance, he wrote: 'I must ask you to convey to members of your orchestra how delighted I was by their performance under my baton.' He did however venture a comment on 'its modest size'. Torquay was clearly trying to establish itself as a centre of musical excellence; unfortunately this was never fully achieved. Hindenberg later changed his name to Basil Cameron; he was the subject of a Question in Parliament. It was reported that it was 'not because he was a German; it was his

A page from the opening night of the Princess Theatre in 1961. The stars included Morecambe and Wise, Tommy Cooper, and singers Joan Regan and Edmund Hockridge.

PRINCESS THEATRE
CONTRACTORS, SUB-CONTRACTORS AND
SUPPLIERS

General Building Contractor	R. E. Narracott & Sons Ltd., Torquay
Site Investigation	Ground Explorations Ltd., London
Piling	Frankipile Ltd., London
Concrete Foundations	James Miller & Partners Ltd., Hayes
Concrete Reinforcement	British Reinforced Concrete Engineering Company Ltd., Bristol
Steelwork	Boulton & Paul Ltd., Norwich
Acoustics	The Department of Scientific and Industrial Research, Watford
Heating and Ventilating Hot and Cold Water Services	G. N. Haden & Sons Ltd., Torquay
Metal Windows	Gardner, Sons & Co. Ltd., Bristol
Copper Roofing	Builders Iron & Zincwork Ltd., London
Felt Roofing	Torbay Flat Roofing Co., Ltd., Kingskerswell
Concrete Floors	Concrete (Southern) Ltd., Hounslow
Concrete Balcony Units	Anglian Building Products Ltd., London
Plastering	A. C. V. Telling (Devon) Ltd., Exeter
Plumbing	A. G. Butchers Ltd., Torquay
Electrical Installation	W. G. Heath & Co. Ltd., Plymouth
Lighting Fittings	Falk Stadelmann & Co. Ltd., London General Electrical Co. Ltd., Plymouth
Stage Lighting	The Strand Electric & Engineering Co. Ltd., London
Stage Equipment	Hall Stage Equipment Ltd., London
Joinery and Bar	T. E. Kennard & Sons Ltd., Newton Abbot
Grilles to Bar	A. L. Gibson & Co. Ltd., Twickenham
Warite to Bar	Fabricated Micas Ltd., Newton Abbot
Glazed Bricks and Tiling	S.G.B. (Dudley) Ltd., Dudley
Glazing	John Hall & Sons (Bristol & London) Ltd., Bristol
Armour Plate Doors and Mirrors	Torquay Glass Works, Torquay
Sanitary Fittings	William Dibben & Sons Ltd., Torquay
Ironmongery	William Dibben & Sons Ltd., Torquay
Precast Stonework	Mexboro & Co. Ltd., Newton Abbot
Main Ceilings	The Expanded Metal Co. Ltd., London
Sound Amplification	Communication Systems Ltd., Bristol
Metal Balustrading	Culford Art Metal Co. Ltd., London
Panelling	Richard Graefe Ltd., High Wycombe
Carpets	Williams & Cox (Furnishers) Ltd., Torquay
Rubber Flooring	Williams & Cox (Furnishers) Ltd., Torquay
Linoleum	J. F. Rockhey Ltd., Torquay
Theatre Seating	Sound & Scene Services (London) Ltd., London
Furniture—Chairs	J. F. Rockhey Ltd., Torquay
Furniture—Tables	Fabricated Micas Ltd., Newton Abbot
Coat of Arms	Allied Guilds, Sutton Coldfield
Il'uminated Signs	Stalite Signs Ltd., Exeter
Stage Drapes	Sound & Scene Services (London) Ltd., London
Refrigeration	W. J. Allsop & Son Ltd., Torquay
Acoustic Tiling	Baileys (Bristol) Ltd., Bristol
Terrazzo Paving	S.W. Flooring Co. Ltd., Totnes

Who did what for the building of the Princess Theatre – a page from the programme on the opening night.

father's name and he (his father) was a naturalised Englishman'. Basil Cameron retained his interest in the orchestra for many years afterwards, appearing as principal conductor on numerous occasions.

The Orchestra struggled on during the World War One, losing musicians to war service as well as having to make other economies. George Bernard Shaw was in the town in 1915 and thought that he was 'swindled', having 'paid two shillings for Beethoven'. He thundered that 'for the bare performance of the notes in the score four horns

Providing some of the music in Brixham between the wars was the Brixham British Legion Band, formerly the Excelsior Band and seen here about 1927.

A 1950s view of Paignton seafront at the end of Torbay Road, showing the marquee that housed entertainments before the Festival Hall arrived on the scene in 1967.

A Torbay Carnival float in June 1966, complete with mock Black and White Minstrels, gently reminding the authorities that Paignton was still without a major theatre. The Minstrels opened the theatre the following year.

September 1975 and work is under way on the new Torbay Leisure Centre at Clennon Valley, Paignton.

[are needed]. There were only two. It requires two oboes and two bassoons. There was only one oboe and one bassoon'.

There were three conductors after Cameron joined the Armed Forces – his farewell concerts took place in May 1916. Those members of the Orchestra not serving in the Forces did charitable work throughout the conflict. For one special concert in the Pavilion some 500 wounded soldiers from the Exeter war hospitals were brought into the town in 115 motor cars and lorries.

Towards the end of the war the orchestra was disbanded and when, in 1921, Ernest Goss took over its remnants, it was said to consist of two violins and a cello. With the active support of the town mayor Goss set about building the new Torquay Municipal Orchestra, remaining its chief conductor until that too was disbanded. Many of the soloists who had appeared at the Bath Saloons now appeared on the Pavilion stage. One was Dame Nellie Melba, who gave her farewell concert there in January 1926. A year later, at the age of 45 Anna Pavlova, the Russian ballerina, gave two performances in the same day.

The Festivals

Under Goss's direction the first Musical Festival took place in April 1930 and similar events continued throughout the 1930s, during which time the orchestra enjoyed a high reputation among musicians and concert-goers. The 1931 Festival programme announced that the Municipal Orchestra, augmented to 50 performers, would have as guest conductors Dr Adrian Boult, Sir Hamilton Harty, Sir Henry Wood, and others. At a subsequent Festival Sir Henry Wood, Sir Dan Godfrey, Dr Adrian Boult, Dame Ethyl Smith and Clifford Curzon all appeared in the same week. Over the next few years these annual events at the Pavilion saw appearances by conductors like Sir Landon Ronald, Eric Coates and John Barbirolli. Noted solo performers included Albert Sammons, Artur Schnabel, Leon Goossens, Cyril Smith and Isobel Baillie.

Situated opposite Torwood Gardens and just across Museum Road from Torquay Museum, the Winter Gardens were an early entertainment venue, until 1903 when the building was sold to Great Yarmouth, where it is still in use.

The Orchestra and individual musicians, particularly Harold Petts (the leader and principal violinist) made regular appearances on BBC radio from Bristol. Arthur Ketelbey was present in person when the Orchestra played a programme of his music in 1938, the second part of the concert being broadcast by the BBC.

Wartime celebrities

In the early days of the World War Two important musical events continued. Both Solomon (who played Beethoven's *Emperor*) and Moiseiwitsch (the piano works of Rachmaninov) appeared on the Pavilion stage. One of the last major musical events of the time was during those dark days of 1940. In May the Tchaikovsky Centenary Festival took place, the Orchestra being conducted on the Tuesday by Sir Malcolm Sargent and on Thursday by Sir Henry Wood. In September 1941 the Dvorak Centenary Festival was celebrated. Torquay-born contralto Astra Desmond was a principal soloist and Sir Henry Wood attended the final concert.

There was another important wartime visitor in 1942 – Sir Adrian Boult, the director of music to the BBC, who had been knighted in 1937. He conducted the Municipal Orchestra which played Mozart, Brahms and the Holst suite, *Beni Mora*. An attempt was made to recreate the atmosphere of the 1930s when 'another great musical event' was arranged in September 1943. This brought the National Philharmonic Orchestra to the town.

Celebrated solo artistes had continued to appear throughout the war years. When Mark Hambourg arrived in December 1941 to give his recital, he was told brusquely at the box-office: 'All seats sold – take your turn in the queue'. Fortunately undeterred, he played works by Chopin and Liszt at the evening performance. It was presented as a 'grand concert on behalf of Mrs Winston Churchill's Aid to Russia Fund'. Campoli had appeared at the Pavilion a month earlier when he played Paganini and Kreisler. This was billed simply as a celebrity recital.

The last days

An attempt was made in October 1945 to revive the annual musical festivals. A Festival Orchestra was even formed. One of the concerts was under the baton of Basil Cameron with Iris Loveridge one of the soloists. The 1946 Festival was conducted by Robert Darrock, Ernest Goss's deputy; there was no festival the following year. The final years' events were modest affairs.

The pianist Moiseiwitsch returned in 1947 and again on Easter Sunday in 1951. A year later, also at Easter, there was a special concert with the soprano Isobel Baillie as soloist. Efforts continued to restore Torbay's reputation for performing music of quality. In November 1953 the Bournemouth Municipal Orchestra played under its conductor Charles Groves, with Kendall Taylor as solo pianist. There were however problems with the numbers attending this particular concert. It was recalled by one observer that when 'Wilhelm Backhaus, then only in his teens, had filled the Bath Saloons in November 1903 [but] the attendance at these concerts is a disgrace to the district… I counted 24 persons in one half of the Pavilion, four in the other half and half a dozen in the gallery'. This was a sad reflection on the lack of interest in classical music in post-war Torbay. A short time later, when Charles Groves was in charge of the 'Bournemouth', concerts for children were taking place in the Town Hall. The Hall was packed and the young people's enthusiasm for the classical performances resulted in applause that echoed around the building.

At that time, in the early 1950s, Torquay Council was having problems balancing its budget. One of the first major casualties was the Torquay Municipal Orchestra. The final concert took place at the Pavilion on Easter Sunday, 1953. Concerts by small ensembles continued to perform for some years but by 1973 these had ended, the Pavilion being used for summer shows only. A further decline in theatre audiences resulted in the last stage performances taking place there in 1974.

It was suggested that the building be demolished, but later in the year it was announced that the building would be 'retained' (a strange word!) mainly through the efforts of Mrs Sheila Hardaway, a conservationist, and her supporters. Subsequently, in 1980, the Pavilion restoration received a top award. It is now owned by Marina Developments Ltd of Southampton; in recent years major work has been done on both the shopping centre's interior and exterior.

Comedies and tragedies

During the 1920s and 1930s the Pavilion also offered popular stage entertainment. Arthur Askey appeared in there pantomime as long ago as 1924. Many other well-known comedians and personalities of the day attracted large audiences at matinées on Wednesdays and Saturdays and at evening shows. In the early months of World War Two the Pavilion became the home of *Twinkle*. This was a concert-party style show produced by Clarkson Rose (famous as a pantomime dame for many years), supported by his wife, Olive Fox.

The war brought important productions from London to the Provinces. In June 1941 *The First Mrs Fraser*, 'St John Ervine's finest play', had Marie Tempest as its star; also in the cast were A.E. Matthews and Robert Eddison.

The concert party era returned to the Pavilion again with Mr Greatorex Newman's Fols-de-Rols popular song-and-dance troupe. The company returned annually for some years.

The Malvern Company

In October 1945, Roy Limbert's Malvern Company presented *This Happy Breed* by Nöel Coward nightly on stage, with matinées on Wednesday and Saturday. During the winter of 1953–4 the Malvern Players were back at the Pavilion with a strong company of actors. The first play, *Relative Values*, was directed by Bernard Archard – when 10 of the 14 actors had parts. Using the stage name of David Baron, Harold Pinter was a member of Philip Barrett's New

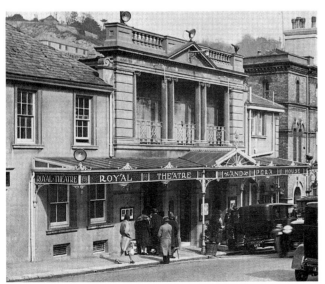

A late 1920s view of the Royal Theatre and Opera House in Abbey Road, later to become a cinema. Taken from the programme of a golden jubilee performance at the theatre in 1930.

Rare picture of Torquay entertainment probably in the years just after World War One. This is the Picturedrome, the town's first cinema, in Market Street (part of the market building) which had become a dance hall and was used for roller skating later. Standing on the right is Vincent Lane, manager, with the band – the pianist on stage was a Mrs Matthews and the drummer was Tommy Knapman. The Picturedrome was used for 'animated pictures' from September 1909, when Mr Mellor was given a three-year lease on the building. It closed in 1935.

Malvern Company which played in Torquay in the autumn of 1956 and the spring of 1957. It is believed that Pinter wrote part of *The Caretaker* whilst at his lodgings and in the dressing room at the Pavilion. Pinter played leading roles in every production that winter. Two Malvern repertory players who went on to play solo roles were Vivien Merchant (to whom Pinter was once married) and Sheila Hancock.

The Princess Theatre

After it had lain half-completed since 1939, permission was given in the late-1950s for the Princess Gardens promenade and theatre project to be completed. This enabled the Princess Theatre to be constructed. It opened in 1961, having cost £180,000. As a municipal undertaking, the Council promised to offer a wide range of choices for its audiences. This was well catered for in the early days.

The Beatles were on stage in August 1963. They were back again later at the Torquay Town Hall. Touring productions from London appeared during the winter in those early days. The London Festival Ballet was at the Princess during October 1964. A month later Anna Neagle was on stage in person (playing in *Person Unknown*). When in 1965 the London Festival Ballet returned, its programme included *Les Syphides* and *The Witch Boy*. These grand offerings did not continue for long.

The arrival of television some years earlier had given prominence to 'personalities' Many of them began to appear, either on one-night stands or as the main attraction for a season. As their popularity waxed or waned through exposure on the small screen many appeared on stage at the Princess; among them were Harry Worth, Val Doonican, Arthur Askey and, in the early 1990s, Jim Davidson.

As part of a deal involving both the Princess and

After the demolition of the Marine Spa in 1971, a new entertainment complex called Coral Island emerged – this was the scene between the two, in April 1974. The old Marine Spa was much mourned and the new complex, aimed at a younger clientele, was never accepted by a large section of the Torquay population. Coral Island opened in 1977 and closed in 1988, the building then becoming almost derelict for several years; following a new round of demolition in 1998, the site was eventually developed as a new attraction in the form of the Living Coasts marine aviary, due to open in 2003.

the Festival Theatre, the Council, in 1991, handed over the running of them to Apollo Leisure, a national operator. Promised improvements included a new, taller, fly-tower above the stage. This failed to materialise in Phase 1, nor was it included in the second stage implemented jointly by the Borough and Apollo during 1997. What was included was a new restaurant on the promenade side, as well as a glazed turret and other improvements and these were all completed on schedule. At the beginning of August 1999 it was reported that

Apollo had sold out to an American entertainment company.

Brass band days

The Royal Italian Band first appeared in the 1880s when Torquay was a Victorian watering place and it was still performing in the new Princess Gardens as late as 1905. Band concerts have remained popular ever since. Between the wars the sounds of brass echoed across both the Torquay and Paignton sea fronts. In the Princess Gardens the military bands performed in a canvas-covered outdoor auditorium. In 1928 the 17th/21st Lancers Band played for four weeks, to be followed by the band of the Cameron Highlanders. A year later the Queen's Own Cameron Highlanders returned, the cost to the Corporation being £175 a week. The concerts were extremely popular and house full signs were exhibited on many occasions. The Torquay Municipal Military Band was formed in 1932 and played in the Gardens in place of the military bands. By 1936 the Municipal Military Band had moved its performances to the newly-built bandstand on Babbacombe Downs. Particularly popular that year in the Gardens was the band of The King's Hussars and the band of the Royal Artillery. Military bandsmen were required by their regiments in 1939 so all these events came to a sudden end.

Visits of brass bands today are usually for just one night. Torbay has its own Torbay Brass Band which appears at various venues around the Bay. Bands of the Royal Marines still give occasional concerts at both the Riviera Centre and the Princess Theatre.

There were military bands in Paignton from 1911. The first performances were in Queen's Park. All concerts stopped during the war years but resumed again in 1919 in Queen's Park. Residents and visitors were promised entertainment by the Royal Marines, the Grenadier Guards and the Oxford and Bucks Light Infantry. A year later the entertainment was moved to a new venue. Paignton Council had erected an octagonal bandstand on the sea front ready for the 1920 season. It was a modest beginning, the Paignton Military Band being the performers. Four years later the Council announced the engagement of a military band (that of the 2nd South Staffs) at a fee of £720. Military bands were back. The chairs inside cost threepence per person (less than 2p). Later the enclosure was surfaced and, in 1926, an awning added. This was subject of much criticism for its ugliness for years afterwards. It led to demands for a proper seafront pavilion, possibly in Victoria Park, but this proposal came to nothing. In 1932 the bands of the Green Howards and the Black Watch were on parade. However, in 1938 the new bandstand was completed in time for a grand opening in April. Its seating capacity was now 1,340 and there was a dance stage. 'The Tent', as it was known, became even larger

when the awning size was further increased. The very popular Herman Darewski was the attraction for some time. The outbreak of war in 1939 meant the end of all entertainments in The Tent but concerts resumed soon afterwards. The bandstand was known as just that until 1953 when the name Summer Pavilion was first used. In 1954 Charles Shadwell and his orchestra were engaged. Tuesday night was talent night, Friday featured community singing and on Saturday there was 'Top Tunes' and a dance competition. Reserved seats cost, 3s, 2s 6d and 2s, an unreserved one just one shilling (5p).

Festival Theatre

In the 1960s there were again demands for a formal theatre similar to the Princess in Torquay, which had opened in 1961. As a result, plans for Paignton's Festival Hall, as it was first known, were prepared and approved. The new building, designed by local architect Mr C.F.J. Thurley, had its gala opening on 10 June 1967 with a performance by the Black and White Minstrels. This show attracted 250,000 patrons during its run. In 1969 it was re-christened the Festival Theatre. In the 1970s and 1980s, entertainers on stage included as varied a selection as Bette Davis, Johnny Mathis, David Essex, Donald Peers and Roy Orbison. There were also occasional visits of ballet companies and concerts by orchestras, among them the Bournemouth Symphony, but the emphasis was always on summer shows for the visitors.

In May 1998 plans were announced to turn the Festival Theatre into a multiplex cinema with 15 screens. Apollo Leisure released its detailed plans for the so-called Hollywood Park film centre in mid-September suggesting an Art Deco appearance with an outdoor terrace. Torbay Leisure Centre and the Palace Avenue Theatre were to be taken over as part of the deal. It was explained that there would be a saving to the Council of £70,000 in running costs and that £1.1 million could then be spent on urgent repairs at the Leisure Centre. The last performances at the Festival Theatre were by the Russian Ice Stars in January 1999. Conversion work began immediately. The new multiplex, Apollo Cinemas, The Esplanade, Paignton, opened on 27 August

The Rosetor Hotel in Chestnut Avenue, just before demolition. The site became the English Riviera Centre, now the Riviera International Centre, giving the Bay a purpose-built conference centre and indoor leisure complex. It opened in May 1987.

1999 with all screens in use. At this time, the future of the Palace Avenue building is in doubt. When it opened in 1880, it had 800 seats.

Live theatre has had a fascinating history in Paignton. The little Royal Bijou staged a world premiere in 1879 when the *Pirates of Penzance* was presented there. It was then apparently 'not much larger than a good-sized drawing-room, tastefully fitted up with oil paintings in gilt frames'. Its successor, created by 'Greta Huggins and friends', used the former stables at the Gerston, seating only 50 when, in the 1950s, it was forced to close down.

Brixham has no purpose-built concert hall. Many local organisations perform in the town hall. The standard of their amateur productions is high and performers and audience deserve a larger auditorium than that currently on offer.

Torbay Leisure Centre

Plans for the Clennon Valley swimming pool were approved in November 1974, building work com-mencing early in 1975, the pool finally opening on 1 July 1976. Torbay had been without a municipal pool since the Marine Spa closed in July 1971. The finished pool was 33.3 x 12.5 metres and the total cost was around £403,000. Over subsequent years, additional facilities were added. The go-ahead was given for the final phase, costing £1.5 million when plans were approved in February 1979. This included squash courts and other facilities. It was then possible for a wide range of sports and entertainment to be held there. By the late 1990s major repairs to the fabric were urgently needed which, as mentioned, the takeover by Apollo had included the promise to undertake.

With the decline of the traditional holiday trade, some kind of major attraction for the 21st century was essential and a highly-innovative Eden Project-type was included in the Torbay Local Plan for the 140 acres between Paignton Zoo and Clennon Valley. Three years later, this remains a pipedream. One recent improvement which was completed was the laying of a new artificial-turf pitch, costing £125,000.

Outdoor activities for all

Public Parks – examples of municipal enterprise – Torquay

MOST of Torquay's public parks were opened by the old Local Board before 1892. These were Torwood Gardens, Ellacombe Green, the Manor Gardens at Meadfoot and Upton Park. The Board had been able to do this partly because the generosity of the Palk family who had given most of the land. The Recreation Ground is still best known because visiting cricket teams use the Torquay Cricket Club's facilities during the season. Rugby has been played there since 1889, except for a short banishment to Plainmoor (when a soccer club offered a higher rent). Originally owned by a private company, it ran into financial trouble and the remainder of the lease was bought by the Town Council for £500. The rates paid for a new grandstand in 1904 (and an extension 23 years later). Ornamental gates of a design worthy of the new Borough, possibly designed by the H.A. Garrett, the Borough Engineer, were erected in 1910, and these are still very much part of the seafront scene. Another of Torquay's local gentry made his contribution. Richard Mallock celebrated Queen Victoria's Diamond Jubilee with a gift of land at Chelston (Victoria Park and Ashfield Gardens)

Torwood Gardens, one of Torquay's first public parks, in the first years of the 20th century.

Torquay seafront's Abbey Gardens, pictured in 1938.

which he wished 'to remain an open space for ever', and Corbyn Head (which came into public ownership in 1906). A third landowner, Mr R.S.S. Cary of Torre Abbey, who possessed land at St Marychurch, also celebrated the Queen's Jubilee by giving five acres there. This has always been known as Cary Park and is still well-used by tennis players and bowlers. The fountain, now rather less impressive than it should be, was given by Mrs R.S.S. Cary in July 1903 in memory of her husband lately deceased. Nearby is Tessier Gardens. It was a gift to the town of Torquay by Mrs H.A. Tessier 'for adults only' in 1933. A Sun Temple was put up later in the year to her memory. This was damaged in a storm in 1990 but was repaired. It has remained a quiet, peaceful place, but the access restriction has angered some people. In the 1960s an attempt was made to alter the covenant but it was then said that an Act of Parliament would be needed. There the subject rested until the summer of 2002 when protests against this archaic rule surfaced again.

In November 1902, Warberry Plantation, covering over 11 acres, was bought by the Council for £1,100 by a loan repayable over 60 years. Warberry Copse, as it has been known ever since, was devastated by a storm in 1990. During the 1990s, after many of the surviving remains of the trees had been cut down, major replanting was done

by the Council with the assistance of local schoolchildren. It will, however, be many years before the damage of that one night is fully repaired.

The end of the decade saw a new encroachment. There was a bitter fight when a proposal was made to site a telecommunications mast at Warberry Copse's highest point. The battle was lost and the mast erected.

Another battle against encroachment was lost at nearby Ilsham. It was finally settled in favour of South West Water, and the building of a filtration plant went ahead in 2002. In 1909 Sir Thomas Bazley, who lived at Kilmorie (now demolished and replaced with a tower block of residential flats) purchased three acres below his house 'to prevent spoliation of the scenery by building'. Mr Palk, whose Manor House and land lay nearby, paid £3,000 for more land, and his gift to the town was endorsed 'to ensure that the beauties of this spot are happily preserved for the public'. More land was bought by the Council later for the same reason.

Abbey Park, one of Torbay's great assets, was just a field leased for grazing when Claude Grahame-White made his historic flight over the British fleet in 1910.

Permission to construct was given in spite of the difficult circumstances that prevailed in the early 1920s. Work went ahead in two stages, the tennis

Sherwell Park in its early days, probably around 1930. The land known as 'Rosery Ground' was bought by the council in 1928 and opened the following year as Chelston Park. Residents were so pleased that they gave a second set of gates and it was then renamed Sherwell Park at their request. Today the scene is pleasantly mature and the stream survives, though the three wooden bridges have given way to more solid stone affairs.

courts coming into use in 1921, the 18-hole miniature golf course two years later, and the whole Park in August 1924. The popular bowling greens date from 1934 when six of the nine grass tennis courts were turned into two bowling greens so that matches and tournaments could be played there. The crazy golf course is a much more recent innovation. Even more recent are the floodlights that make evening play at tennis possible.

Upton Park dates from about the same time. Looking at its trim and ordered form today, it is difficult to believe that this is all land-fill and that well into the 20th century the open River Fleet flowed along the bottom of the valley below where the bowling green stands. There was another bowling green and a putting green, both now long since gone, further up the valley. In 1993 a new sports pavilion was erected and what was described as a vandal-proof fence put up at the same time.

There was a US Army field-kitchen in Upton Park in the months before D-Day. Large numbers of GI's, sleeping in nearby houses, could be seen day after day queuing for their chow. The old huts were in the news again in 1946 when squatters were in occupation, demanding accommodation from the

authorities. More recently a large holding tank was constructed underground for water which builds up during flash storms. There are now no visible signs of the tank's existence and few people would know it is there. Other works to reduce town-centre flooding are at Hele and Ellacombe. Floods still occur in Union Street from time to time. The problem remains only partly solved.

Chelston has two parks; Sherwell Park is on what used to be called Rosery Ground, Mallock Road and Armada Park is on high ground above Cockington. When the Rosery Ground was bought in 1928, it comprised two parcels of land. It was decided to keep the northerly part undeveloped and use it as a playground for children. Fenced in and with the latest play-toys, it is still one of the safest places for them to play. When the other part was laid out and opened, the residents in Lower Chelston were so pleased with its appearance that the Council given a second pair of gates as a gift. These rather elaborate gates still grace the southern entry to the park. Armada Park was opened officially in 1956. As well as a large football pitch (still well-used), swings were provided. These too have now been fenced in and modern equipment for children installed. In

The Torbay Archery Club in session at Queen's Park, Paignton around 1912. The later picture shows the Mayor of Torquay in 1949, Alderman Fred March, extreme right, receiving guidance when an archery club at the Shiphay Manor Hotel attempted to revive the sport in Torbay.

1999 plans were announced to sell off part of the park for house-building. This caused great controversy and the building development scheme was subsequently removed from the Local Plan. Permission, however, was given for a mobile-telephone aerial to be erected at its highest point provided it was disguised as a fir tree. This was completed in April 2001 and is just one more of the strange modern sights that have become part of our landscape.

Kitson Park in neighbouring Shiphay opened in 1966 as a small adventure playground. It was named in memory of the late Major R.F. Kitson whose family had done so much for the parish.

Public Parks – Paignton

When the Gasworks closed at Hollacombe, the future of the land seemed in doubt. After some delay the Gardens opened on 3 April 1981. The *Herald Express* reported that it had cost £382,915 to complete the work, £203,915 for the land and £137,500 for the landscaping

On the south side of Torbay Road lay Mr Kellock's Marshes. This was acquired for an open space and its layout started in 1900 when '3,000 tons of earth were bought at 10d a load delivered'. The official opening of Queen's Park was in 1901 and it was used immediately for many different events. Band concerts were arranged and the Archery Club had their shoots there. Paignton Rugby and Hockey Clubs were given sole rights to play there in 1908. The bowling green and pavilion were completed and opened in 1937. It has been said that today life continues much as before.

Victoria Park was completed just before the end of the 19th century – in time for the Agricultural Show to take place there in 1900. The park, as we see it today, took many years to complete. The final setting-out was not done until 1937. Today the only remaining part of the ancient marshland is a small plot behind Paignton Library. This was constructed on a concrete raft in 1961, after the final portion beside Courtland Road had been filled in. In 1971 the nine-storey Victoria Car Park was built beside the railway, replacing the hard-standings that had been there since the 1930s.

Public Parks – Brixham

In 1938 Brixham Council bought two fields near St Mary's Church for £1,160. The original plan provided for tennis courts, a football pitch, bowling green and so on. In 1939 the Castle Playing Fields plan was a subject of much criticism. It was said that there was 'a crying need for sewage work, improvements to harbour and breakwater but money was being frittered on a white elephant nobody wanted to ride'. In spite of the onset of war it was possible for the recreation ground to open on 1 June 1940 with some of the facilities promised earlier, including the bowling green. Brixham Bowling Club, formed in 1914, played at Furzeham. The first bowling green in Brixham had been opened there in June 1913.

Paignton Zoo

The story of Herbert Whitley and Paignton Zoo starts in 1892 after the death of his father, a Liverpool solicitor, and his mother's decision to invest in land in South Devon. The family arrived in Paignton in 1904. At Primley House, and at the house next door, the family began breeding dogs including greyhounds and whippets in 1912. Monkeys joined the menagerie and the first exotic birds arrived a year later. Shortly before the end of the war, in 1918, Herbert Whitley's family of cockatoos had full liberty and flew up freely around

Torquay racecourse at Petitor in 1914. The course had seen action since 1864 and it continued until Easter 1939. The Torquay and South Devon Golf Course began life on the same land in 1909.

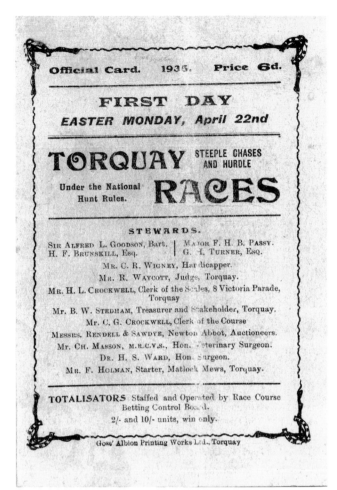

Official Card. 1935. Price 6d.

FIRST DAY
EASTER MONDAY, April 22nd

TORQUAY RACES
STEEPLE CHASES AND HURDLE

Under the National Hunt Rules.

STEWARDS.

Sir Alfred L. Goodson, Bart. | Major F. H. B. Passy.
H. F. Brunskill, Esq. | G. I. Turner, Esq.

Mr. C. R. Wigney, Handicapper.

Mr. R. Waycott, Judge, Torquay.

Mr. H. L. Crockwell, Clerk of the Scales, 8 Victoria Parade, Torquay

Mr. B. W. Stedham, Treasurer and Stakeholder, Torquay.

Mr. C. G. Crockwell, Clerk of the Course

Messrs. Rendell & Sawdye, Newton Abbot, Auctioneers.

Mr. Ch. Masson, m.r.c.v.s., Hon. Veterinary Surgeon.

Dr. H. S. Ward, Hon. Surgeon.

Mr. F. Holman, Starter, Matlock Mews, Torquay.

TOTALISATORS Staffed and Operated by Race Course Betting Control Board.
2/- and 10/- units, win only.

Goss' Albion Printing Works Ltd., Torquay

From a 1935 Torquay Races racecard; owners' names such as Paget and Mildmay show that some of the top people frequented the meeting.

3.50—4th RACE (GREEN ARMLETS)

The **West of England Handicap Steeplechase** of 70 sov. (60 sov. to winner, 7 sov. to second, and 3 sov. to third): the winner, after the publication of the weights (April 11th, at noon), of a handicap steeplechase to carry 7lb. extra; entrance 2 sov.; two miles. (10 entries)—Closed March 26th, 1935.

AGE ST. LB.

1 Miss Dorothy Paget's ... ... **FIREWORK** aged 12 7
   blue, yellow hoop, yellow cap, blue hoop (Snow)

2 Capt. W. R. West's ... **PHALDARILL** aged 12 3
   white, scarlet cross belts and cap (T. L. Hall)

3 Mr B. Warner's ... ... **SANDRO** aged 12 2
   orange, black seams, black cap (O. Anthony)

4 Mr A. B. Mildmay's ... ... **YARMOUTH** aged 11 9
   white and blue hoops, white sleeves, quartered cap (H. E. Whiteman)

5 Mr J. Dennistoun's ... ... **ARDROWAN** (dr.) aged 11 8
   green, buff cross belts, halved cap (T. Rayson)

He had a similar brush with the authorities in August 1937 when he was again charged with failing to collect entertainment tax. This time he was fined £25 with 10 guineas costs. Forward-thinking in many ways, in June 1927 Whitley had offered the zoo as an educational facility, and the 1s 2d admission for adults included tax; children, however, continued to be charged only 6d. For some period it appeared that the zoo would have to close, and its animals be divided among other collections. In 1934 the Council was negotiating to buy, for £9,000, part of Clennon Valley for a sports ground. This land was adjacent to 14 acres which included Clennon Gorge (then undeveloped) which was owned by Whitley. He generously gifted this to the Council so that a larger area could be developed. There were plans for 22 tennis courts, nine football pitches and a grandstand but, because of the onset of World War Two, the land remained undeveloped until the Torbay Leisure Centre was built at the seaward end. World War Two played an important role in safeguarding Whitley's venture. In 1940 many animal evacuees from Chessington Zoo were re-homed in Paignton. The zoo also benefited from sizable investment and improvements in conjunction with Chessington. In 1939 there was a moment of excitement when Ben, an Indian leopard, escaped. Paignton was under siege for some days until on 12 January Major Simon Yorke, a former Mountie, killed it with his first shot.

Whitley died in 1955 and the Herbert Whitley Trust was set up soon afterwards. Subsequently, after delays and much discussion, permission was sought to build a supermarket on vacant Zoo land and, *quid pro quo*, the Trust would have funds to maintain and improve the Zoo itself. After going to appeal, the plan was approved in October 1994. The new Safeway finally opened in May 1996.

As a result, and with £2.9 million from the European Regional Development Fund, a major development was put in hand. The plans included a new entrance building that came into use in 1996. Later, in the spring of 1997, the Marie le Fevre Ape Centre was completed. It was opened officially by the Duke of Edinburgh on 23 July 1998, having cost £750,000 to build (of which £500,000 had come from the lady's legacy).

In September 1997 the Zoo opened its new

the district. Herbert opened Primley Zoo (as it was then more usually known) in 1923, the commercial aspects of which were of little consequence to him. Possibly to limit the number of visitors, he made a charge of 6d (3p) per child and the 1s (5p) for adults for walking along his private road. There were no other charges. However, in March 1924 he was summoned by Customs and Excise for not levying entertainment tax – something he steadfastly refused to pay. He was brought before the local Bench and fined £1 with 10 guineas (£10.50) costs.

Torquay Bowling Club's greens close to the entrance to Princess Pier. The club had started out on the Recreation Ground in 1892 but an escaped elephant from Wombwell's Menagerie wrecked the greens.

Watching a Brixham regatta opposite the Breakwater, in 1937.

mammal house (for elephants and giraffes). It was part of the new 'savannah habitat' plan. The Zoo obtained a great deal of publicity when the BBC chose it as the location for a popular animal series – *The Zookeepers*. A purpose-built veterinary centre was opened in June 2002 by Noel Edmonds, the well-known broadcaster now resident in the West Country.

Further ambitious schemes are included in the next five-to-ten year programme but these are subject to assistance from the EU and elsewhere.

The Model Village

In April 1963 Mr Tom Dobbins opened his model village on the slopes behind the St Marychurch

shops; it was based on one he had owned at Southport. This has been developed extensively over the past 40 years and is now a major attraction of international importance.

Outdoor sports in the three towns

These have attracted participants and supporters over the past century and a half. Rugby has remained popular with players, but the numbers of spectators are fewer than those of 60 years ago. Brixham RFC play at Astley Park. Their future was secured when Mr B.A. Astley sold the ground to Brixham Council in 1933 for £500 'on condition that rugby could be played there for ever'. Torquay Cricket Club was founded in 1851. History records

A-class yachts at sea in the 1962 Torquay Regatta.

that a cricket match was played at Furzeham in Brixham to celebrate the Fall of Sebastopol in 1855 but little else seems to have been written about a cricket club in the town until early in the 20th century.

Other sports and clubs have done likewise and Torbay's only professional football club, Torquay United AFC, entered the Football League in the 1927–8 season. The club was formed in 1899, by old boys of Torquay College and Torbay College, and they eventually played in the Eastern League, later known as the East Devon League. As an amateur club they played at Teignmouth Road, Torquay Recreation Ground and Cricket Field Road before spending four years at Torquay Cricket Ground.

In 1910 they moved to their present home, Plainmoor, and in 1921, still known as Torquay Town, they merged with Babbacombe FC and became Torquay United, turning professional and being formed into a limited company the same year. They first joined the Football League in the Third Division South and over the years have moved between the Third and Fourth Divisions. In 1956–7, United were pipped to promotion to the Second Division on goal-average by Ipswich Town. That season they went unbeaten at home. In 1989 they were runners-up in the Sherpa Van Trophy.

In May 1924 a Davis Cup match was played on the tennis courts in Abbey Park. It was against Belgium with the home country winning by a narrow margin. More than a decade later, in 1936, Fred Perry, perhaps the greatest male tennis player this country has yet produced, played an exhibition match there before a crowd of 2,000. It was in the same year that the covered court, described as the finest in Europe, was opened at the Palace Hotel. In the post-war years Mr Arthur Roberts became resident coach there and among the stars he made were Joan Curry (a National Covered Courts champion), Angela Mortimer (Wimbledon champion in 1961) and Sue Barker who, after a distinguished playing career, established herself as one of the BBC's best-known television presenters.

Horse Racing

Going to the races in Torbay is now only a distant memory. The first course was not far from Torquay

On the Torquay harbour slipways, E-class boats prepare for action in a regatta event in 1963. The slipways had been built by American forces in 1944 as part of the preparations for the D-Day landings in Normandy.

The 1950s cycle track at Watcombe, close to the chimneys of Watcombe Pottery.

United's present ground and racing started there in the 1850s. The annual event moved to Waddeton at Churston for a few years before settling at Petitor in the 1880s. In 1946 it was reported that 'the National Hunt Committee would allocate the meeting to Wincanton or elsewhere in the south west. It would be difficult to get it back'. It never did and the Torquay Golf Club has been in sole occupation ever since.

Today there are no locations around Torbay that are large enough to cater for the great numbers of enthusiasts who follow their favourite sport and the area's future as a major sports centre appears to have gone for ever.

From gas lamp to the electric light

WITH the arrival of the electric light in the very first year of the 20th century, the people of Torbay saw, arguably, the technological revolution that changed their way of life more than any other. In March 1900 Torquay councillors were told that 'there are now 214 consumers using electricity'. They had what was described as '10,033 8-candle-power lamps'. Two years earlier, when the generating station was commissioned on Beacon Quay, there had been just 55.

The Torbay towns lighted by gas

The story of gas (or 'Town Gas' as it should be more correctly called) started in Torquay in 1834 when the first gas-works opened in Torwood Gardens because it was 'so far removed from any houses'. The works were later moved into the town centre and subsequently to Hollacombe in 1861. The well-lit streets today, almost all from dusk to dawn, are taken for granted. The situation in Paignton a

A fine aerial picture showing the gas works at Hollacombe. The site nearest the bay was closed in the mid-1970s and eventually became gardens, with circular ponds taking the place of the two gas holders. The last gasometer, the largest, was demolished in 2003.

century ago has been recorded in some detail. Before 1900 street-lights were 'fish-tails with naked flames', and the 'incandescent mantles' that gave a brighter light were only introduced with reluctance (although they appear to have been less costly). The lighting of the lamps was let out on contract with mixed results. Two years later lamplighters appeared to be sub-letting the work and there were complaints that children were lighting and putting out the lamps. As late as 1905 gas supplies were only available in the built-up area of Paignton. It was not until after World War One that gas lamps in the streets began to be changed over to electricity. But even then much of the area lagged behind. As late as 1928 oil street lamps between Tweenaway and Collaton were being converted to gas, never mind electricity.

Much earlier, St Marychurch (until 1900 a quite independent place) was very unhappy with the gas supply it was getting from its larger neighbour and decided to build, as a piece of municipal enterprise, a gasworks on Babbacombe Beach. Fortunately this plan was still-born, but an official application to Parliament by the Local Board of Health was successful and permission was granted to construct a plant in Barton Hill Road. This opened in 1869 and it continued to produce gas until the late 1920s.

After it was sold in 1926, it was agreed that the proceeds should be used for the good of the parish. A new bandstand was built on Babbacombe Downs with some of the money and later Anstey's Cove was bought with some of the remainder.

Brixham first had a gas supply in 1838. In 1872 it was reported that 'the mains are in a bad state; although much had been renewed, between 100-200ft of gas an hour is being lost through the old pipes which still remain. Supply during the day is bad or non-existent and there is only half-pressure at night'. In the first decade of the 21st century, it is just possible that some of those old pipes could still be in place.

The population explosion had taken place in Torbay in the last decades of the 19th century and most of the houses had a gas supply fitted as standard; this continued to be used as the main source of light for many years.

In 1948 the gas industry passed into public ownership and the South Western Gas Board came into existence. The Hollacombe Works continued to make gas until 1969. The arrival of safer 'North Sea Gas' meant the old way of extracting it from coal was no longer necessary. Later the industry was privatised as British Gas plc.

This 1961 picture of the Hollacombe gas works, adjacent to the main Torquay-Paignton railway line, shows just how massive the operation was – not quite what was wanted on the seafront of a major resort.

Another view of the gas works, this time as the backdrop to a maritime incident in which a Danish freighter, the Northwind, ran aground close to Hollacombe beach in December 1964. The ship was on her way to Teignmouth to load china clay and was refloated the following evening.

The last traces of the 150-year-old gas-making plant disappeared when the large gas-holder opposite Hollacombe Gardens was demolished in 2003.

Switching on the electric light

Electricity was entirely a 20th century arrival and totally a municipal enterprise. The Borough Council was given authority to generate electricity under an Act of 1891. The Borough formed an Electric Lighting Committee and it decided that the principal generating station should be beneath the Bath Saloons at Beacon Quay as the boilers were fired with sea-borne coal and there was plenty of water for the condenser. Growth was so fast that in 1902 additional equipment had to be bought. The current supplied was alternating current but the trams, which arrived on the scene in 1907, ran on direct current. Another generator for this purpose

was installed and resulted in many complaints about the increased noise, dust and dirt. The Imperial Hotel took the matter to the High Court but the action failed. As a result the Council promised to remedy the smoke nuisance from the chimney. Demand increased enormously in the next decade and a half and a new generating station, away from Beacon Quay, became essential. The new municipal power station was opened at Newton Abbot in September 1924, the works at the harbour having closed shortly before. When conversion from gas to electricity took place in many of the older properties in the 1930s the cost per unit was just over one old penny. It had not changed for some time. Costs rose during World War Two and, mainly because of inflation, rises have continued ever since.

The positioning of a power station at Paignton brought plans for a generating station in Queen's Park; land near the harbour was also considered. After the Council made a promise in 1903 that

Brixham gas works after a German air raid in May 1941.

Torbay's new power station at Newton Abbot opened in 1924 and decommissioned in 1974. It is seen here as a fine backdrop to a busy railway scene in the 1950s.

Paignton was to be illuminated by electricity, it took five years to agree that the Electric Light and Power Company should be the public suppliers from a generating station behind Dartmouth Road. There were just eight customers at first and they first received electricity on Christmas Eve in 1908. A few weeks later the first electric street lamps were put up. It was several years before gas lamps were replaced by the electric light, since the Gas Company had a 10-year agreement to supply gas for the lamps ending in 1915. The position remained unchanged for ten years until 1925 when Paignton Council made attempts to buy the company. However, at about the same time Torquay Corporation began negotiations to supply electricity in bulk. This was agreed late in the year and Paignton became part of the Torquay supply area. Soon after, the generation of electricity ended, the plant closing down in February 1926.

Paignton had been on direct current from the very first days but the equipment at Newton Abbot produced only alternating current. Special rectifiers had to be installed for DC (direct current) to continue to be supplied until the conversion to AC (alternate current) was completed. That took five years. In 1935 Torbay was connected to the National Grid.

From 1911 Brixham Gas Company also began supplying electricity. The works were in the centre of town, the generator resting on 200 tons of concrete. This caused severe vibrations in the properties nearby and in 1913 was the subject of a legal action against the Company. Among the witnesses for the appellants was a Dr Young, the local GP – later better known as Francis Brett Young, the novelist. As late as 1923 the village of Churston was still without electricity and approaches were made to the Brixham Company for a supply as far as Churston Station. When this was finally done is not known.

Under the Electricity Act of 1947 the industry was nationalised and in 1948 the whole of Torbay became part of SWEB's operation. The power station at Newton Abbot closed down in about 1975 and was demolished soon after. All supplies now enter South Devon by the Grid. South West Electricity became SWEB plc in 1989.

Decline and fall – Torbay's industries

Shipbuilders at Brixham and Galmpton

THE name which still conjures up memories of a great Brixham shipbuilder is J.W. & A. Upham, founded in 1817, or earlier. In the 1890s the works and yards covered three acres. The slipways could deal with vessels up to 400 tons burden. In 1926 *Vigilance* was the last Brixham fishing smack built there. In July 1939 Upham's new Dry Dock opened; it measured 150 x 50ft. The greatest use made of it was during World War Two. Between 1939 and 1945 over 1,000 vessels were built or repaired for the Government; the beach on the sea side of the breakwater was also used. Among other contracts, the yard built 13 vessels of the Fairmile design. After the war, perhaps the best-remembered of Upham's projects was the construction in 1956 of *Mayflower II*. Like its predecessor and namesake, which carried the Pilgrim Fathers to the New World, it made its epic journey across the Atlantic, reaching the United States in July 1957.

The only evidence of a very long-established shipbuilding industry (trawlers built near the spot were first offered for sale in 1783) is the memorial plaque to Messrs Upham unveiled by the builders Midas in July 1999.

Robert J. Jackman and his four sons established a shipyard on Breakwater Beach in the 1850s. Work continued there until about 1912 when it moved next door to Upham's. *Terminist* was the last trawler launched from the old yard. Vessels continued to be built on the Jackman slipways nearer the town until *Sevabo* was launched in 1927, and this was possibly the last of its type ever built locally. The day of the tan-sailed trawler was over. The yard had become derelict by the mid-1930s.

Galmpton has had a long history of shipbuilding, mostly trawlers but not totally so. William A. Gibbs yard was taken over by

Launch of the *Terminist* in 1911, the last trawler to be built at Jackman's Breakwater shipyard in Brixham. Pictured below are the men who built the *Terminist*.

A 1950s view over the old boat quay at Brixham harbour, as a Western Lady ferry arrives. In the centre background can be seen the Uphams shipyard and the waterfront which became the site for the Prince William Quay apartments development fronting the new marina.

J. W. & A. UPHAM
BRIXHAM
P. A. UPHAM, Proprietor

Awarded Silver Medal and Diploma of Honour, 1883

Ship and Boat Builders
CABIN CRUISERS
COMPLETE INSTALLATIONS AND REPAIRS
Spar Makers & Ship-Smiths

Good accommodation for the laying up of small Yachts and Motor Boats for the Winter Months

A business postcard of Upham's shipyard – note the 'Awarded Silver Medal and Diploma of Honour, 1883'.

The shipyard scene at the time of closure in 1988.

Sanders & Co before 1906 and its yard remained working for over 30 years. *Provident* (still afloat) was launched from the yard in 1924. She had taken six months to build; the timber for her hull had been seasoning nearby for ten years.

There was a great fire at Galmpton in 1933, and the smoke and flames could be seen across Torbay. It was reported that moulds lost were part of the shipbuilder's stock-in-trade. They had been accumulated for the better part of a century and represented the art of several generations of shipbuilders. Although Sanders remained in business, there seems to have been no further launches

This round stone, looking rather like a giant doughnut, was one of the mementoes to be taken across the Atlantic in the *Mayflower II*. The card says the stone was from the Berry Head House home of the Revd Henry Francis Lyte, who wrote the famous hymn, *Abide With Me*. The stone was to his memory and that of the 344 Brixhamites who died in the two world wars. 'It will be transported to America on the Mayflower and be built into the Cathedral of the Pines in New Hampshire, which contains memorial stones from all parts of the world'. The reverse of this rare postcard says that the Flanders poppies adorning the cushion are 'given by Pinhoe Exeter British Legion'.

reported. Stanley Hall of Galmpton Kiln, on the north side of Galmpton Creek, built 15 Fairmile-design vessels for the services. The Torbay Boat Construction Company still has its small yard on the south side. The quay can accommodate a Western Lady during overhaul but the resumption of any ship or yacht building on any scale in the future at Galmpton seems unlikely.

Paint-making in Brixham

Making paint at Brixham began in the mid-19th century after a valuable iron mine was discovered in a

The Torbay Paint Company works in Brixham, which employed 80 people, closed in 1961. The works provided paint for the ironwork in London's Big Ben clock tower.

Watcombe marble works in 1961 and the managing director, Major Godfrey Grant, holds one of three white onyx caskets being made for scrolls presented to new Freeman of the Borough that year. A sheet of onyx, marked out, can be seen in the foreground as Mr Jack Black cuts another over the water tank. Grant's had been established in 1830 by Major Grant's great-great-grandfather. The onyx, a white marble, was imported from California.

Company. Although its main offices were in London, it had works and mines at Brixham and Dartmouth. The celebrated Torbay Paint, as it was known, was used all over the world for bridges and viaducts, piers and lighthouses, palaces and county mansions, museums and art galleries, among others. It also produced enamel and heat-resisting paints. By the 1920s Messrs Pinch and Johnson were the owners of the now-renamed Torbay Paint Works. The company remained in business until the late 1950s when the firm was bought out by Courtaulds. Paint manufacturing in Brixham ended soon afterwards. The samples of

field belonging to Mr Samuel Calley in New Road, Brixham. The ore was found very near the surface, and a shaft sunk which yielded an abundance of mineral. By the beginning of the 20th century the New Road operation had become the Torbay Paint paint weathering on metal sheets were a familiar sight on Rae Hill for many years. During World War Two, at its works in New Road, Torbay Paint made millions of gallons of camouflage and other paint for the Navy and the RAF.

Longpark Pottery in Torquay – the chimney was originally built for Brunel's atmospheric railway system. Right: Some of the machinery looked decidedly primitive.

Marble

In the past there were some fine local marbles quarried in South Devon but by the start of the 20th century almost all the stone was being imported from overseas. Walter Jenkins & Co operated from premises in Lymington Road for over a century (latterly becoming part of Building Specialists Ltd Group of London). The company concentrated mainly on larger-scale work although the factory was still making decorative objects from Ashburton marble as late as 1966. Their massive water-lubricated cutting saws, which seemed to be working day and night, were for many years a familiar sound in Upton.

After World War One, Jenkins & Co received the hugely important commission of building the Canadian National War Memorial at Vimy Ridge in France. The foundations were designed by Oscar Faber but the memorial itself was the work of the Canadian architect and sculptor, Walter Allward (1875–1955). He personally searched Europe for a suitable stone and eventually found a quarry at Trau in Yugoslavia (that had not been worked since AD 295–305 when its stone had been used for Diocletian's Palace at Spalato). His plan to use an Italian workforce for the work failed to materialise because of local labour difficulties and so the erection was eventually carried out by Frenchmen and Belgians employed directly by the firm. They did all the work except the sculpting of the figures; that was the responsibility of Luigi Rigamonti. The *Torquay Times* reported that 11,285 names had been engraved; these comprised 102,508 letters and all were sand-blasted individually by Mr Kernick, a craftsman from Torquay. Work on the memorial began in 1921 and took 15 years to complete. The memorial was unveiled on 26 July 1936 by King Edward VIII, one of the few formal duties he undertook during his short reign.

The firm went into liquidation in 1996 but continued trading for a further year. The *Herald Express* reminded its readers that 'over the years it has done work at Oldway, the Imperial and Grand Hotels; also for the London Hilton and for Saudi Arabian princes'. A small industrial estate subsequently took its place.

Potteries

It is ironic that although no pottery pieces are being made in Torquay today, its past efforts have attracted interest around the world. In 1996 the Torquay Potteries Collectors' Society celebrated its 20th

'Phone: 63220

LONGPARK POTTERIES

NEWTON ROAD TORQUAY

JUST a reminder of your visit to the Longpark Potteries, which we sincerely hope you have enjoyed, and if so, we shall esteem it a great favour if you will be good enough to make known to any friends of yours who are likely to be coming this way that there can be seen (free of charge) the manufacture of real Devonshire Pottery from the raw state to the finished article.

HOURS OF INSPECTION:
9.30 to 12.30   2. to 4.30 p.m.
Saturday, 9.30 to 11.30

Buses pass the Potteries every ten minutes and will stop by request just by the gates. Plenty of Parking room for cars and coaches

Managing Directors:
GEORGE W. BOND   FREDERICK H. BLACKLER
ROBERT H. SKINNER

Promotional postcard from Longpark Pottery.

Fixing spouts and handles at Longpark Pottery, after shaping the 'slip' (finished clay).

anniversary by publishing a definitive work telling the history of all the South Devon potteries but, more importantly, illustrating both in colour and black-and-white the finest pieces of local red terracotta clay made in the 20th century. The story starts in the late 19th century when red clay was discovered in the grounds of Watcombe House during building operations for its owner, Mr G.J. Allen. At first the clay was sold to other parts of the country but a decision was made not long afterwards to erect a pottery nearby. Watcombe Pottery began operating just at the right time; art pottery was increasingly in demand – and was to remain so for the next 30 years. The main object was undoubtedly to provide employment for the people of St Marychurch. The position was explained thus: 'The directors are not mere speculators, who would sacrifice any amount of reputation for gain [but] are gentlemen very intimate with Art'. Production ended in 1962, by which time Watcombe Pottery produced everything from terracotta angels to advertisements for soap. In later years its products were mainly for the holiday trade but the variable quality of some of the designs has not deterred collectors worldwide. Brian Reade, a Torquay man who became Deputy Keeper at the Victoria and Albert Museum, recalled that his father, Thomas Reade and George Bedford, both art-teachers but also fine artists, did

part-time work for Watcombe in their younger days. Brian Reade's personal collection of terracotta pieces was donated to the town of his birth (and is on exhibition at Torre Abbey).

Red clay was also found at Hele. As a result the Torquay Terra Cotta Company came into existence. The clay was dug from a pit in the middle of the site and two kilns were later built near the Gas Works. When the demand for unglazed pottery declined, the Company made glazed ware, marketed and marked as Crown Devon Ware. It was later renamed Torquay Pottery and, in the 1920s, was usually referred to as the Royal Torquay Pottery. It also used the mark Hele Cross Pottery. It continued to produce a wide range of wares up until 1939. By the end of the war parts of the building had become a laundry and ceramics were never made at Hele again. For some years there was another pottery nearby. The Mayville or Barton Pottery was established in Barton Road (the premises are now occupied by the Co-operative funeral establishment). Barton produced good designs but these have since been criticised as old-fashioned. Barton Pottery closed down sometime before 1939.

A prominent landmark still visible on the skyline at the side of Riviera Way is the Longpark Pottery chimney. This was built originally as a pumping house for Brunel's South Devon railway but was never used as the 'atmospheric caper' was

Biscuitware after first baking.

abandoned in 1848 before any machinery was installed. During the first decade of the 20th century it called itself the Royal Tormohun Pottery. In about 1914 it seems to have changed its name again, this time to the Royal Longpark Pottery. It is best known for its kingfisher and cockerel patterns. The pottery closed down in 1957 and is now the home of a fruit and vegetable warehouse.

The depression years of the 1930s started the decline and when business began to return to normal after World War Two only Watcombe, Longpark and a few small potteries remained operating. Working local red clay finally ended when Watcombe closed down in 1962.

It has been said that the workers in the smaller potteries were mainly copyists, but the experimental work done by Lemon and Crute at the Daison Art Pottery was not all copied by any means. Harry Crute ARA seems to have painted kingfishers – a design claimed by Watcombe but used mainly by Longpark. When asked where he obtained his clay, Harry told his enquirer that there was plenty to spare when graves were being dug at the cemetery nearby. Over the years the kingfisher was copied throughout the West Country. The Torquay decorators did, of course, move from pottery to pottery just

The Watcombe pottery chimneys are demolished following closure in 1962.

The Torquay Pottery factory at Hele, almost opposite where the *Herald Express* building is now situated on Barton Hill Road.

The Torquay potteries made many everyday domestic items and also a variety of fine, elegant pieces such as these decorated vases, which have become collectors' items around the world.

The STC factory at Paignton on its then greenfield site in the late 1950s. Below: Some of the first workers.

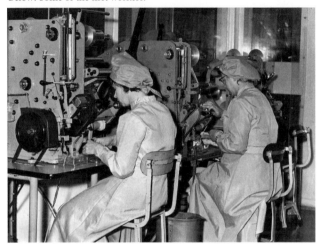

as had the earlier Staffordshire craftsmen, from whom some had descended.

Brick making

The same rich red clay so popular with the potters also made fine household bricks. Right up until the 1960s many houses built in Torbay were constructed with these local products. In the 1920s there were two brickworks in Paignton. The Western Counties Brick Company had its large Western Works in Brixham Road and Webber and Stedham (later trading as Western Counties Brick Company) had their works adjacent to Paignton Zoo. In 1969 a private developer was given permission to erect a warehouse on the Western Counties Brickworks site. This is now a well-established business. The former Primley brickworks near the zoo is the location of the Safeway super-store mentioned earlier.

At Torquay the Western Counties Brick Company had its factory on the Newton Road near Lawes Bridge – the smoking chimney and rattling conveyor belts were a familiar sight and sound there. Its products were still so much in demand that, in 1958, a new laboratory was opened to test the strength of

the bricks and blocks made by the Company. Yet within a decade all local brick-making had ended. In 1963 it was announced that brick-making would shortly end at Old Woods. The demolition of the chimney followed a year later. The small Woodlands industrial estate now occupies most of the old brickworks site.

Precision engineering

Standard Telephones and Cables (STC) set up its factory off the Brixham road in 1957. As part of Paignton Council's desire to bring new industry to the town, housing and other help was given to the so-called incomers. The whole Valves Division was moved from Ilminster. As the plant was conceived and built during the Cold War it had its own air-raid shelter. It was near a hill so that manufacturing could be transferred underground. Over the next three decades the Company prospered and the STC factory expanded and developed on land nearby. It also leased the old water-mill at Bovey Tracey; the Rotunda and other buildings at Oldway were used for training purposes from 1954 onwards.

Later becoming Northern Telecom (and later still

The Sifam factory in Woodland Road, Torquay in 1971. Below: Inside the factory's glass partitions working area.

Nortel) a £12 million investment was completed in April 1994. The next development caused criticism. When the new 16-metre high building was nearing completion its stark whiteness was visible for miles around. Prince Michael of Kent opened the enlarged factory at the end of April 1997. The first 500 redundancies were made in 1999 when the Company abandoned undertaking commercial telephone work. The last five years have been disastrous for the Nortel workers in Paignton. In the autumn of 1998 business conditions were said to be so bad that much of the factory was empty with every possibility that it would remain so for months. Matters had, however, improved by February 2000 and the Paignton factory which had been empty for some months was again in use. Shortly after, the *Herald Express* reported that 'the operation has prospered and 4,500 were employed on specialist products for the internet industry. A further 250 workers have been recruited to meet increased production now that $1.2 billion was being invested by the Company worldwide'. The

Timber boats in Torquay harbour in the late 1930s.

A scene from Torquay harbourside in the 1930s when there will still a considerable timber trade with Scandinavia.

equipment being brought down in pantechnicons and set up in the empty buildings. Key staff lived, as well as worked, at Leigh Court as Tudors School, as it was called, had been a day and boarding school with large playing fields and gymnasium. The factory remained there until the new purpose-built works were completed in 1960 on the Woodlands Estate off Barton Road. For many years it specialised in the manufacture of small meters and other components for industry. However, in November 1999 it was taken over by the North American-based JDS Uniphase for £60 million, as it was then principally involved with making fibre-optic components for telecommunication systems. The company at that time employed 200 people but the *Herald Express* said that 'this was expected to double in the next 12 months'. In February 2000 the Company said that it was still intending to expand its operations but less than two years later, like many other hi-tech industries it was reducing the scale of its operation. Like Nortel the situation became worse and in September 2002 it shut down completely. A new company, Sifam Fibre Optics, began operations in October 2002. Its work was said to be 'of international importance'.

whole business ran into serious trouble early in 2001 and there were massive redundancies in two 'tranches'. There were more in July. The decline in demand for electronic products continued after September 2001 and even more were necessary. Those at Paignton were almost total and in the autumn of 2002 the company's optoelectronics division was sold to Bookham Technology of Abingdon.

A small family company has also played an immensely important role in the development of electronic instruments. In 1940 Sifam moved into Leigh Court, a former school in the Lincombes. James Patrick Mackenzie, the owner, had been forced to leave London because of the blitz, the

Quarrying at Berry Head, from a postcard sent in 1960.

The changing workplace

IN THE mid-1890s two young Americans came to England and, for some reason not fully explained, came to Torquay, travelling around Torbay for several weeks. It is strange that the only known first-hand account of working conditions in Torquay a century ago should come from the pen of a young American, Isabella Cowan. Early in 1893 she wrote in her diary: 'The tradespeople give their employees 2 weeks vacation every summer and dis-

miss them every Wednesday at 4.30pm. Their regular hours are from 8am to 7.30pm with the usual extension during the holiday rush. They seem to have little reason for the strike for shorter hours that is premeditated now, although their wages may be as low as their hours are short. Mrs Mills (their landlady) pays her girl 3s or 75 cents a week. Those who sew get about 5s'.

To our modern sensibilities Miss Cowan's

Opening day for the Marine Drive at Ilsham in 1924 – a scheme to alleviate unemployment.

In the early years of the century working conditions for children were still bad – but at least in Torbay they could escape to the beach, as shown from this Meadfoot scene in an early 20th-century postcard.

assertion that workers in Torquay had little to complain of seems somewhat unfair, yet we should remember that her comments reflect as much her time as they do her personal attitude. This was, indeed, a shorter working week than had been customary: only 20 years earlier, the 12-hour day (from 8am to 8pm) had been granted. Cabbies worked a seven-day week (much longer even than most other workers) so that people could go to church on Sundays. For this long toil, they were still paid only a few shillings.

As late as 1900 the working conditions for young children were still very bad. A news item read: 'For a lad of 11 to carry 24 quarts of milk daily, for another boy of the same age to toil as an errand boy before, between and after school hours until 11pm on a Saturday, 49 hours a week for a miserable pittance of 2s 3d is sweated labour of the most glaring sort'. Mr Roberts, headmaster of Upton National School gave examples of boys working for a greengrocer in the lunchtime; they had no time for eating, the pay

was 2s a week for one, 2s 6d for another. Even worse off were the young dairymen! One boy of 12 worked from 6.30am to 9.30am, 4.30pm to 5.30pm and all day on Saturday until 10pm for 1s 6d a week and his breakfast. 'Not even a glass of milk was given!'

David Lloyd George had become Chancellor of the Exchequer in 1908. A year later old-age pensions were paid for the first time; to many claimants they had the nickname of 'Lloyd-George'. Those whose applications had been allowed had been given books containing 25 cheques or orders. Those with incomes of less than 8s (40p) received 5s (25p) and those with incomes of more than 10s 6d (53p) nothing. One delighted person said: 'No workhouse for me now'. The state pension was limited to people over 70 who had been British subjects of 20 years. The weekly amount was later increased to 10s. (The age did not come down to 65 until after the 1925 Act.) The 1930 Poor Law Act made only the aged and infirm eligible for the workhouse. However, for many years elderly people continued to fear 'being

Even in the later 20th century there was still campaigning to do for some youngsters in Torquay. This is the old Queen Street in 1963 when mothers were petitioning the council for a play area, the street having become too dangerous for leisure activity.

A fine shot of the corner of Victoria Street in the town centre, showing the site now occupied by the Tesco Metro store. Laurence Pile Foale stands in the doorway of his shop in 1907, he having established a prosperous family business, combining it with Home Park Farm at Goodrington. The site shown here was known as Foale's Corner as late as the 1960s.

sent to the workhouse'. Indeed, to this day newspapers print memories of poor folk who grew up in institutions.

Two years later in 1912 a report read that the 'Perseverance Tent of the Independent Order of Rechabites had 50 new members initiated at one time, due to the impending operation of the National Insurance Act'. It was only just over 90 years ago that the first official steps were being taken to look after the sick and unemployed working people. There were several other non-profit organisations offering what they termed as security for a small weekly payment. That idea was developed by William Beveridge in 1942 and formed the basis for his Report that resulted in the National Health Service we take so much for granted today.

World War One, and the inflation which followed, did not improve conditions greatly. A surviving Williams and Cox's Fines Book from the early 1920s shows that the situation of 'shop-girls'

had changed little. The entries show that fines were levied in some cases for what seem to us to be trivial offences:

Filling in index incorrectly	*2d*
Late down from dressing time	*6d*
Altering customer's bill without explanation	*1s 3d*
Omitting to credit goods	*2s*
'Entering charge of 19s 6d twice'	*2s*
Leaving the Department	*2s 6d*
(a quarter of a week's wages)	
Carelessness in packing parcel	*2s 6d*
Late arrival at business	*2s 6d*
Marking goods the wrong price	*4s 6d*

There were 41 fines recorded in the two years covered by the book.

Working for the gentry

Most girls found employment in the large houses that had been built from the 1830s onwards. To occupy them in their short leisure time and keep them away from the 'demon drink', provision somewhat similar to the British Workman (a public house without liquor) was made for them at the Christian Alliance for Women and Girls' building, located at the junction of Union and Fleet Streets. This remained open until 1960 when it was demolished to make way for the island near the GPO. The CAWG still has a holiday centre in Ash Hill Road.

A young Elizabeth Cleave joined the staff of Normount in 1919 as a kitchen maid. She tells us that the indoor staff comprised: a lady's maid; cook/housekeeper (this was a modest staff; earlier, some houses had a housekeeper, cook and assistant cook); butler; parlour-maid; head housemaid; second housemaid and kitchenmaid. The outdoor staff in 1919 were: head gardener; coachman and groom (he was later renamed the chauffeur when the motor car arrived) and two under-gardeners. (Other large houses in the Lincombes and Warberries had footmen as well.) Miss Chadwick, the owner, like other maiden ladies, also had a 'companion'. These were often 'gentlewomen in reduced circumstances', who in reality were often little more than servants themselves – attending to every whim of their mistresses!

She continues: 'At mid-morning the carriage-and-pair would arrive at the front door, the horses well-groomed, the men wearing hats with cockades'. A Frith photograph of the time shows a carriage on Paignton sea front, resplendent with a footman as a standing postilion! Many local girls became servants since it was the only work available. Boys became errand boys or worked in the gardens of the grand houses.

In the *Millennium Story* for the *Herald Express* I included a childhood memory which told how life had continued unchanged in the big houses right up until the late 1930s:

'My maternal grandmother, Grandma Pope, was a widow before she was 40. There was no State help in those days so she went back "into service" in one of the great mansions in the Lincombes. My mother became a cook at quite a young age in a large house nearby. Aunt Ida served a five-year apprenticeship as a dress-maker and tailoress. I earned my pocket-money delivering my aunt's completed commissions. One of her customers was a Miss Stack-house whose father, a general, had been one of those who had put "Great" before Britain whilst serving his Queen in India. She lived, with a modest staff of about eight, at Lanark Lodge in Woodend Road. Another was Miss Chamberlayne, also the daughter

Bringing the goods to the people – a Paignton Co-operative Society van pictured on the Foxhole estate possibly in the early 1960s.

of a general. General Chamberlayne's exquisite watercolours of India have become much sought after by collectors. They graced the walls at Las Flores in Ash Hill Road where she lived, right up to the outbreak of World War Two. Her long-serving staff had grown old with their mistress.'

Out of work and on the dole

Unemployment became a problem soon after World War One. In 1921 the Mayor set up his Fund for the Relief of Unemployment – subscriptions were listed weekly in newspapers. The Marine Drive was constructed with aid (£1,780) from the Unemployment Grants Commission. The years of the Depression which followed shortly thereafter are often thought to have had their worst effects in industrial areas but poverty was also bad in Torquay. In 1931 the Winter Relief Soup Kitchen was opened in a converted garage in Pimlico by the Mayor.

A report ran: 'Presiding over the ladies was Mrs H. Richman. A competent chef and under-chef had been obtained from the Labour Exchange. The first person to arrive for the soup was a pinched looking young man who, on that cold day, had no overcoat, collar or tie. £150 will be needed to keep the Kitchen going through the winter'.

There was also a travelling depot providing soup outside St Paul's School, Plainmoor (12 noon), St James's School (12.20) and at the Hele end of Salisbury Avenue (12.40) each weekday. The soup kitchen was run by a committee; representatives included those from the Council of Social Service, British Legion and the League of Help.

The Department of Social Security, and the Benefits Agency that is now part of it, started its work 50 years ago as the Ministry of National Insurance. This was set up by the first post-war Labour government and introduced major changes in both working conditions and social welfare. The first offices in 1949 were set up at Cleave Court in the Warberries. The choice of location for those first offices was often questioned. Cleave Court was isolated and not easily found. However, the house had been requisitioned by the War Department in 1944 and probably the reason why the new Government department was placed there. After six years the first move was made to Torwood Gardens and later to the purpose-built offices on the site of Cotswold in Warren Road.

The first Labour Exchange in this part of Devon was opened in the Burlington Arcade (opposite the Old Town Hall) as long ago as 1910. Larger premises were required and it soon moved to 27 Fleet Street (opposite to where the GPO stands today). After World War One the return of the ex-Servicemen increased the work so much that a further expansion was needed, the Albert and Struben halls then being taken over.

During the Depression in the 1920s and 1930s long queues of the unemployed formed outside the Employment Exchange (as it was by then called) in Albert Road. This moved yet again. The Jobcentre provided the Department of Employment's new image in the town whilst the larger premises at Roebuck House enabled claimants to queue under cover. In the mid-1990s the Unemployment Benefit Office (UBO) and the Jobcentre moved to Regal House (built on the site of the former Regal Cinema), replacing both the UBO in Abbey Road and the Jobcentre in Market Street.

As the 20th century closed there were still signs that 'the poor' existed in Torbay. A survey made in early 1996 indicated that in 45 percent of homes in the Barton, Hele and Watcombe districts no one in the household had a job.

At home in Torbay

Home Fires Burning: those at home in wartime.

ALTHOUGH the Royal Navy had anchored in Torbay over the centuries, most of the sailors had remained on board. If granted shore-leave, as 'pressed men' they would have 'disappeared into the hills behind the town'. The first time Torbay folk saw men-in-uniform was during World War One. In late 1914 large numbers of troops were quartered in private houses before going to France. A rhyme current in 1915 promised the military:

> *Three meals a day for the men must be fed*
> *Each man a pound and a quarter of bread*
> *One pound of meat at a shilling a pound*
> *And one pint of beer must be found*
> *Four ounces of bacon and two of cheese*
> *With two pints of tea – milk and sugar please*
> *Then when night-time comes a separate bed*
> *Can it be done do you think for a fee*
> *Of Two and Three.*

From the start of hostilities the amount paid to householders billeting troops had been 2s 3d per day or 15s 9d per week but, for some reason, those in some parts of Torbay had been allowed more. However, from 1915 all British towns billeting troops were paid just the 2s 3d by the War Office. The verse above, published in the *Torquay Directory*, shows what had to be made available to them. The allowance was not nearly enough, complained the householders. Urgent requests were made to London for an immediate increase. No evidence of the outcome to this demand has been found. Wartime governments are not so easily moved.

At the end of 1914 hundreds of men of the RAMC were billeted in Torbay. In Torquay at the same time were 900 Irish soldiers of the 1st Dublin Fusiliers 'who paraded through the streets in tropical gear'. They were among those who landed at Gallipoli a few months later. Only 40 survived of the 1,100 who went ashore. Different accents and strange uniforms were filling the town later. Between 1917 and 1919 some 29,000 New Zealanders were repatriated from Torquay. As they were 'in batches just passing through', they were accommodated at the Daison, Hampton Court and other large properties in the town.

Those of us who experienced it remember well the food shortages endured in the early 1940s when the Battle of the Atlantic was being waged, and more ships containing food were being sunk than were arriving safely at British ports. We forget, though, that food was scarce many years earlier. In 1918 allotments were set up in Victoria Park, Paignton, Sandringham Gardens, Orient Road and elsewhere. Dig for Victory was as important then as it was during World War Two. The main crops grown were potatoes, the seeds having been bought in bulk by Paignton Council.

Two decades followed when arrivals were mostly holidaymakers coming for a week or fortnight by the sea. However, in the late 1930s strangers were reported to be secretly 'buying up large houses' in the district. They were of course the many Jewish families fleeing from persecution in Germany and Austria. *The Jewish Chronicle* reported in October 1939 that '125 families are residing in the area with about 75 children who will need religious instruction and the provision of Kosher meat'. This

Wounded Belgian soldiers being hosted in Torquay during World War One. The date is October 1914 and they were being taken on a sightseeing tour. One of the tram advertisements relates to the Picturedrome cinema.

was a matter of serious concern to local Jews. Matters of even greater concern to those who had fled mainland Europe were developing. The first Enemy Aliens Tribunal was held in Torquay Town Hall on 30 October 1939. About 30 aliens of German and Austrian nationality and 'mainly of Jewish extraction appeared before Mr Justice Thesiger to state the reasons why they should not be interned'. The appellants were 'more male than female and were all residents in the Torbay area'. Most had come 'since the Nazis took power' and included a banker, a doctor, a former German Criminal Court judge and a schoolmaster. The proceedings were not open to the Press or public so its decisions were not known. No later sittings seem to have been reported, possibly because censorship was being introduced more rigidly as the weeks went by. Some of those who were sent for internment went to the Paignton camp on the edge of town. It was a so-called privilege camp because although those resident there were compulsorily interned, they contributed to the cost of being kept there. High security fences were put up and a guardhouse erected at the entrance. The chalets were occupied by Germans and Italians. Their dislike of each other was so intense that dividing barricades had to be put up to keep them apart. A similar camp was set up at

Seaton and, sadly, many of these inmates were drowned whilst being transported to Canada on the *Arandora Star* which was torpedoed off Ireland by a German U-boat. It is likely that some of the Paignton internees were among those who died.

Wartime evacuees

After the Fall of France the number of evacuees, mostly unaccompanied children, arriving in Torbay increased greatly. Many of those sent from the big cities in the autumn of 1939 had returned home, so this was a fresh influx. The Billeting Officer for Torquay and his staff worked tirelessly to get the children into homes, many having to be billeted with families unwilling to have them. One reluctant householder commented: 'The children billeted on me were very unmannerly and hooligans. I shall not take any more'. There had been considerable price inflation between the two wars and in May 1940 the Government announced that allowances would be increased: for children aged 10–14, 10s (50p) a week; for those aged 14–16, 12s 6d and all those over 16, 15s (75p). The young evacuees, mainly from the London area, arrived by train at both Torquay and Paignton stations. The children had set off from their schools dressed in school uniform and

There was no shortage of activity on the Home Front in Torbay during World War Two. Pictured here are women in October 1941 coming back after raiding the countryside for rosehips, to help with the food supply, and, below, sitting in a garden rolling the webbing for camouflage nets in late summer of the same year. This group called themselves The Rollers.

Not the least of the activity on the Home Front was that of the Home Guard. This unidentified and undated picture shows one of the local battalions marching along Vaughan Parade, long before it was ever thought of for today's pedestrianisation. The presence of an RAF cadet suggests this picture was no later than 1943.

carrying a gas mask in the regulation cardboard box. Each was allowed to take one small bag (or carrier) which contained spare clothing and underwear. Every child had an identification label pinned on coat or jacket. Those coming to Torbay left either from Paddington or Waterloo. Some of those who took in the children were shocked at their shabby appearance and lack of manners. They arrived tired, crying and very hungry. In July compulsory billeting again was necessary when 550 boys and girls from Plumstead and Woolwich arrived in Torquay. The *Torquay Directory* reported that 550 children had come earlier and that a further 400 from London SE district were expected.

In July 1940, the billeting officer at Paignton had to deal with 1,795 children and 170 adults who all arrived in one day. Brixham was still only a small fishing town but a report in the *Brixham Western Guardian* confirms that it played a major part when the 'town's complement was 699 children and 58 adults who disembarked from trains at Churston and were taken into the town in Devon General buses'.

These evacuee youngsters' fancy dress parade in Torquay in 1942 was all part of the war effort – two of the posters on the left declare 'Let us push her to victory' and 'Join our savings group and buy your savings stamps here'.

Belgians in Brixham

Many Belgians found refuge in Brixham in both wars. Large numbers arrived after their country had been overrun by the Germans in 1914. Most returned home afterwards but their fishermen continued to use the port between the wars – and some worked from it. Early in 1940 when the German Blitzkrieg swept through Holland and Belgium, a large number of them left Ostend intending to go to Dieppe, 'but finding it already in enemy hands, sailed on to Brixham and Salcombe,

Evacuee children, mainly from the London area, arrive at Torquay railway station in July 1940 in a bid to escape the forthcoming enemy bombing. Note the apprehension in their faces – and the necessary comfort brought by a favourite doll.

complete with their families, relatives, friends and household possessions'. The number of vessels in that fleet varies depending on which account is read. It may have been as high as 250. Adults and children were accommodated all over the town. When the families were about to return after the Liberation in 1944, a less comfortable story of their arrival was retold:

'Trawler after trawler moved into the Outer Harbour foodless, waterless, the refugees possessing only what they stood up in with men, women and children crying out "We want food, We want bread…" Brixham eased their hunger and thirst… emptying the bakehouses, the grocers' shops, the dairies so that every packed trawler received a real welcome in their dire distress. Trawlers entered the port with decks, topsides and sails scarred with bullet-holes. Babies were born on the incoming trawlers. The Belgian children were methodically educated under Belgian teachers by the Devon County Education Committee. Outstanding results

in proficiency in English resulted. The children also spoke fluent English and sang English popular songs and the National Anthem'.

Eleven of the Belgian fishermen had lost their

Visitors to today's Torbay are often surprised to discover that the area suffered any bombing at all during World War Two. In fact, the Three Towns suffered 264 raids in total, which cost 196 lives.

WVS members and friends at Ellacombe repair dungarees and tunics for the armed forces during World War Two. This group met at 'the old bowling hut' led by Mrs George Dyment, who is fifth left in the back row. The women also knitted socks and balaclava helmets.

lives through enemy action or through mines while fishing out of Brixham. Some of these Belgian families remained in the town and descendants are still resident.

Bombs in the South West

During the Blitz many lives had been saved by the Anderson shelters that had been dug into the gardens. After the Fall of France, the likelihood of being bombed existed throughout Britain and in the summer of 1942 Morrison and Anderson shelters were delivered to homes in Torbay; Paignton alone was allocated 2,805. The *Paignton News* told its readers that 'Morrison indoor shelters would be issued free to those employed in an occupation compulsorily insured under the NHI Acts and whose earnings did not exceed £350 p.a. Others could purchase them for £7'. Torquay homes had them supplied as well. Less than a year later the air-raid danger was over in South Devon and in August

1944 it was announced that the shelters would be collected by the Council and sent to London. The attacks by Hitler's terror weapons, the V1s and V2s, had just begun to rain down on the Capital.

Just a little earlier, at the end of 1943, many residents had been evacuated from South Hams to Torbay. This was to allow the Slapton Sands area to be used by troops practising for the Normandy landings. Many stayed with friends, but others had to be found temporary homes. Because of the numbers of properties already full, this was not easy.

Scenes reminiscent of World War One took place at about the same time. Billeting officers in Army uniforms (United States, not British this time) began knocking on doors, mainly in Torquay and Paignton, seeking temporary lodgings for the thousands of American troops who began arriving at Liverpool and other ports from the end of 1943 onwards. Many were were found billets in local people's homes – and were fed in field-kitchens set up in public parks around Torbay.

Upheaval in mid-century – the GIs arrive

ABRIEF entry in a Royal Air Force station logbook at the Grand Hotel in Torquay records under the dateline 29 January 1944: '1,500 United States troops, in transit, fed in relays by the Wing'. These were the Americans who were on their way to Slapton Sands to set up a beach-landing base. They were the forerunners of the many thousands who came to Britain over the next six months.

It may be argued that the 'Slapton Story' began in peacetime. In 1938 Brigadier Montgomery, as he was then, was given the task of arranging an invasion exercise at Slapton. The 9th Infantry Brigade landed from primitive landing-craft under the watchful eye of Swordfish aircraft from *HMS Courageous* anchored offshore. In October 1943 a huge US supply base was established at Exeter covering 95 acres. It was from there that food and supplies were issued to the many thousand troops quartered across the South West Peninsula, prior to taking part in Operation Overlord. The official US account explains that there were 1,100,000 soldiers, 124,000 sailors and 427,000 aviators in Britain by early June 1944, many of these in the West Country.

Two US Army units later produced written accounts of their experiences in Torquay. The 3204th Quartermaster Service Company was housed in properties, large and small, in Chelston. A history of the company published later in the USA

Early in 1944 the American troops began to mass in the Torbay area, preparing for the invasion of Normandy. This young lady found that getting to the beach was impossible. This photograph, originally taken by the *Torquay Times*, was published in 1989 in a *Herald Express* 'Bygones' publication called 'Our War' marking the 50th anniversary of the start of hostilities. The newspaper had no idea who the young woman was... but on publication the paper's well known countryside columnist, Brian Carter, identified the bather as his mother-in-law, Carol Littlewood.

recorded in some detail where the men lived and the friends they made. Large houses used by them included: Cypress Heights, Brierley and Cockington

Mrs Mary Thairlwall, Mayor of Torbay, unveiled a plaque commemorating the building of Torquay harbour's D-Day hards and their role in the Normandy invasion. The ceremony took place during the 40th anniversary of the invasion in 1984. A similar plaque was erected at Brixham breakwater, where the American forces also constructed hards.

The D-Day hards soon became an accepted part of the harbour and proved most useful. This is during the Torquay Regatta fair of 1950.

Vicarage. Among the smaller terraces occupied were those in Sherwell Lane, Rathmore Road, Avenue Road, Old Mill Road and Tor Park Road. The other unit was the 618th Ordnance Ammunition Company, 6th Amphibious Engineers. Bob Perry from Concord, California survived the battle in Normandy and kept in touch for many years with his Torquay hosts. Bob noted that he 'drew a single at the intersection of St Marychurch Road with Forest Road called Brooklyn Villa'. Others were in small terrace houses in Upton and Plainmoor. For several months in early 1944 the 6th Engineer Brigade were also in Torbay. They were billeted in a holiday camp at Paignton.

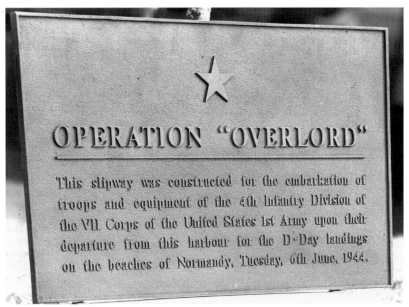

The plaque commemorating Torbay's role in the D-Day preparations of 1944.

The D-Day Hards

In the harbours of both Brixham and Torquay concrete 'hards' (the latter became Grade II* Listed by English Heritage in June 2000) were built by the men of the Royal Engineers. Temporary piers were erected so that infantry men could embark directly on to Assault Ships. At Brixham several houses near the harbour were demolished after just five days notice so that the large US Army tanks and other large vehicles could turn the sharp corner near the breakwater. On 29 May 1944 a German news agency broadcast announced: 'Torquay was the object of last night's raid on Britain. Formations of heavy bombers dropped large numbers of incendiary bombs on the harbour installations'. However, a few days later thousands of US troops embarked without incident.

Caring for the wounded in three

IN Torquay and Paignton the local gentry were encouraged to loan their large residences as convalescent hospitals for the wounded of the South African War. In February 1900, through the efforts of the MP, Richard Mallock, and his wife, Villa Syracusa on Daddyhole Plain became the Syracusa Convalescent Home for Invalided Soldiers. By the time it closed in December 1901, 225 men had been patients there. At Paignton Mr Paris Singer made a similar gesture. In January 1900 he then owned Redcliffe House. This was fitted out as a convalescent home, providing 20 beds with room for ten more patients.

Almost as soon as war was declared in 1914, the local gentry again allowed their large residences to become convalescent hospitals. The Hon Mrs Burn, wife of local MP Colonel Burn, offered Stoodley Knowle at Ilsham for use by officers wounded in action. This was ready within a month and the first patients arrived on 1 October 1914. There was an X-ray Room and Operating Theatre. A Swedish masseuse was in daily attendance for massage and electrical treatment. By the end of 1915, some 319 patients had been treated and 80 operations performed. Other mansions were soon being used,

Paignton seems to be en fête for the departure of this train load of soldiers early in World War One. They may have been some of the hundreds of RAMC personnel who were temporarily stationed here late in 1914.

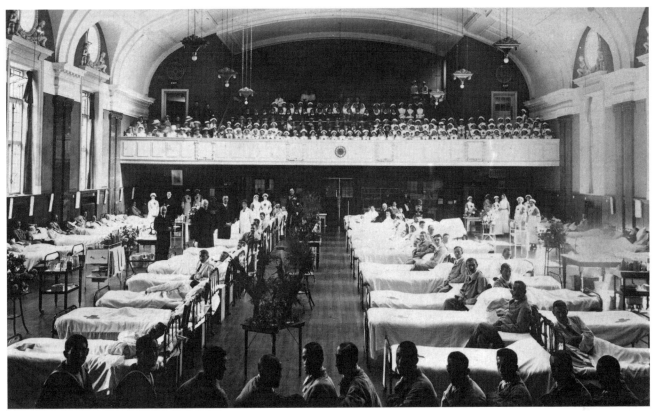

A fine view of Torquay Town Hall during World War One, when it was a First-Line Hospital.

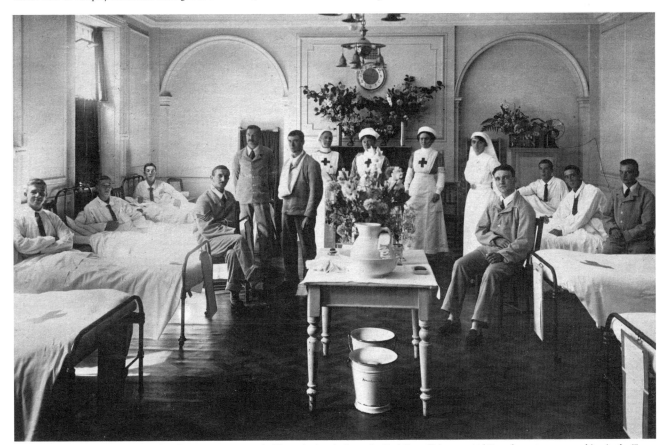

This postcard was marked being of the 'Torquay VAD Hospital' but whether it shows the Red Cross Voluntary Aid Detachment nurses working in the Town Hall or one of the large houses nearby is not clear.

Rockwood, for example, becoming an overflow hospital for the Town Hall. Officially called the Red Cross Hospital, it opened on 21 October 1914 with 50 beds, the first patients arriving the same day. This was strictly for Other Ranks. Officers were taken to Stoodley Knowle as soon as they left the ambulance trains. When the Torquay branch of the Red Cross Society was set up in 1908 three Voluntary Aid

A fine picture of Oldway Mansion in its World War One guise, with nurses making the most of the surrounding land. On the right can be see the Rotunda and below is a rare interior picture of this building in its hospital dress.

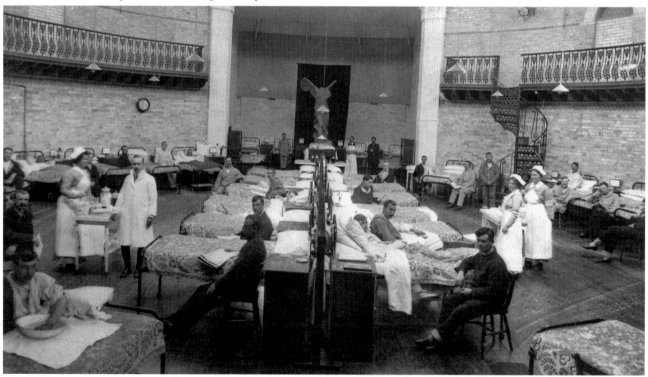

Detachments were recruited from its members. When the call came six years later, VAD nurses provided most of the staff required. The Town Hall was a first-line hospital, receiving most of its patients who had been wounded overseas, although some beds were available for troops stationed in the town and men from the Australian and New Zealand armies were also hospitalised there later in the war. The *Torquay Directory* in October 1914 reported: 'To the Hon Mrs Burns Red Cross hospital for officers has fallen the honour and privilege of receiving the first contingent of wounded officers in Torquay. Most of the 130 wounded soldiers in the American Red Cross Hospital at Paignton are making a satisfactory and in some cases a rapid recovery'. All the wounded soldiers, many on stretchers, had to be transported from the Torre railway station so five motor ambulances and a trailer were obtained. Local tradesmen made their delivery vans available as ambulances when necessary (no account of how the patients fared has yet been found!). The Red Cross Hospitals for Other Ranks closed officially on 31 March 1919. The statistics are impressive. In all 6,323 wounded had been treated and 1,540 operations carried out. As well as using the new Town Hall, patients had been accommodated in temporary wards, wooden huts erected in the nursery field behind. Many years later this was filled in to become the site of the town centre car park. In April 1919 the full story of the part played by Red Cross hospitals was published. It named all those working there and included that of '3rd Dispenser, Mrs A. Christie (part time) 1914–1919'. Agatha Mary Miller had married a handsome young officer, Archibald Christie, on Christmas Eve 1914, home on leave from the RFC in which he was serving as a pilot. After enrolling in a first-aid class, Agatha, now using her married name of Christie, became a volunteer nurse at the Town Hall hospital, working there for two years without pay. She subsequently became a dispensary assistant in the Torbay Hospital (now Castle Chambers) nearby. She worked there for two years, later obtaining a Society of Apothecaries diploma. It was there that she acquired her knowledge of poisons that was to become such an important feature of her writings. Agatha Christie only twice invented fictitious poisons. Common poisons used by her murderers included, we are told: strychnine (in *Mysterious Affair at Styles*); cocaine (*Peril at End House*); barbituate (*Lord Edgware Dies*); digitalis (*Body in the Library*) and morphine (*Sad Cypress*).

Oldway as a war hospital

As he had done a decade earlier at the Redcliffe, Paris Singer immediately made Oldway available as a hospital for war-wounded, leasing it to the American Women's War Relief Fund. He became vice-chairman of the Hospital Committee (Lady Randolph Churchill was the chairwoman) and personally supervising its conversion. It was a surgical hospital with 200 beds and was quickly accepted by the War Office (through the British Red Cross Society) on 21 August 1914. It had a first-class operating theatre, a radiographic studio, pathological laboratory and anaesthetising and sterilising rooms. All this was ready by the end of September 1914 and when the first casualties arrived most 'were able to mount the waiting GWR buses unaided. The more seriously wounded were removed on ambulance stretchers and carefully placed in vans. Only one casualty died enroute from Southampton, his body was removed at an intermediate station'.

For some time members of the American Red

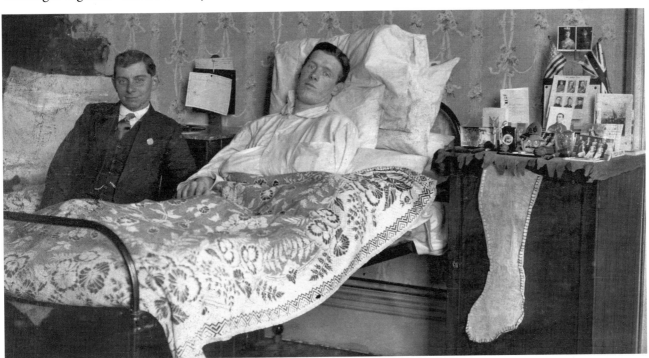

A touching scene inside Oldway during World War One, with a patient hoping to celebrate the forthcoming Christmas with the aid of a stocking optimistically hung on the bedside cupboard. Note the pictures of the King and Queen.

The Palace Hotel in Torquay in its days as an RAF hospital, showing the severe damage caused by the October 1942 air raid which killed 19 people.

Cross worked there (the medical and surgical staff were all Americans) but most were recalled in October 1915. From November it was staffed with American surgeons, an English matron and both English and American sisters. At the time of the Somme offensive 255 beds were ready. A 1916 report formally recorded the help given by the Paignton folk. It read: 'To all members of Paignton Fire Brigade who have never missed attending at the Railway Station on the arrival of a convoy to act as Volunteer Stretcher Bearers, no matter what time of day or night they may have been called upon'. The 'Patrol of Boy Scouts' gave similar assistance as messengers. Paris Singer used his contacts to encourage wealthy Americans to endow beds. Among those well-known philanthropists donating £100 and therefore entitled to name a bed were: Mr and Mrs Andrew Carnegie, Miss Mary Dodge, Mr E.H. Harriman, Mrs H.C. Hoover, Mrs Marshall Field, Mrs F.W. Vanderbilt, Mrs Whitney, Mr S.R. Guggenheim. Three had 'Princesse Edmond de Polignac' printed on the inscriptions above them. Winnaretta Singer, sister of Paris, had married Prince Edmond in the early 1890s.

A Mrs Mitchell was a voluntary helper at Oldway in 1915. She invited soldiers recuperating there to write in her autograph book about their experiences while on active service. It has been said that many ex-servicemen kept their ordeals in the trenches to themselves, refusing ever to talk about them. Mrs Mitchell seems to have been more successful. The distress he had suffered was fresh in the mind of Private C.M. Butcher of the 2nd Hampshires (29th Division). He wrote: 'I left Devonport for the Gallipoli Peninsula on 15 May and arrived there safely after a monotonous voyage of three weeks'. Butcher was soon under fire; even on the beaches they were subject to Turkish shell fire and while in the firing line he suffered a heart attack. After a spell in Malta, Butcher was returned to the United Kingdom in the hospital ship *Asturias* and was sent by train direct to Oldway. Rifleman A. Edwards of the 2nd Battalion Kings Royal Rifle Corps took part in the first battle of Ypres and later 'was sent to Armentieres and was in the trenches with the Indian troops. At Givenchy I was in an advance and then, after a retreat, was back to the old position when a shell burst in the transverse where five of us were, four of them were killed and I was the only one to come out alive'. He was sent to Paignton with a large shrapnel wound and a bullet in his side. There is another account that tells of the writer being 'one of the few left who were not killed or wounded that day so I fought on'. That too was at Gallipoli. A common sight in World War One were the wounded soldiers in 'hospital blues' walking our streets.

Little is recorded about American servicemen in Torbay during that war. However, there were recorded deaths in 1918 at the Oldway hospital. In one week alone 100 servicemen died there. The bodies were first buried in Paignton cemetery but were later exhumed and taken back to the USA.

The Palace, Torquay, as a war hospital

War-wounded were back in Torquay early in World War Two. Torquay's Palace Hotel became a recovery hospital for RAF officers until October 1942 when it was severely bombed. It had been set up in 1939 with 48 beds; by December that year the number had risen to 249. Several hundred aircrew, including some of those shot down in the Battle of Britain, received treatment there. The hospital staff then consisted of 11 RAF officers, 87 other ranks and WAAF, 22 members of the RAF Nursing Sisters (including a matron and four senior sisters) and 83 civilians. Many former staff of the hotel continued to work there. Four second-floor bedrooms were converted into a theatre block. This work was completed in May 1941.

In July 1941 the hospital had a visit from the Princess Royal. She talked to a pilot of Coastal Command who told her that he crashed into the sea when flying back from escorting a convoy, how he was badly injured and trapped in the cockpit of his sinking aircraft. His injuries were so bad that he was initially presumed to be dead. She met also Polish and Czech wounded men and one American pilot wounded whilst flying with the RAF.

At the time of the raid on the Palace there were 203 in-patients, the hospital being full. Casualties were recorded officially as: 19 dead, one missing and 45 injured. One bomb scored a direct hit on the east wing, the west being blast-damaged by a near-miss. Two members of the Home Guard in the street nearby also died in the raid. The building was left under a care-and-maintenance party but during a second raid in January 1943 the central block was damaged; there were however, no further casualties. The badly-damaged building was abandoned and remained derelict for a number of years.

New techniques to help the recovery of the severely-burned were devised there and some of the patients survived for many years afterwards. Among

One of the RAF personnel bombed out of the Palace Hotel in 1942 was Dan Maskell, then the Rehabilitation Officer and later to find fame as an England tennis player and commentator on BBC television. He returned to the hotel in 1975 to unveil a plaque to commemorate the wartime years. With him is Leslie Lownds Pateman, the then president of the local branch of the Royal Air Forces Association, which erected the plaque.

wartime aces who recovered at the Palace were Richard Hillary (author of the classic book, *The Last Enemy*), Squadron-Leader 'Bill' Simpson (the badly-burned pilot who wrote *One of our Pilots is Safe*, also a 1940s best-seller) and the only RAF VC of World War Two, James Nicholson. He had delayed baling out to shoot down another German aircraft and needed the skin-grafting skills of Archibald McIndoe to aid his recovery. He heard of his award whilst riding up to his room in the lift there. Returning to battle, Nicholson was killed in action in the Mediterranean. Dan Maskell, who went on to become a well-known tennis commentator, was the Rehabilitation Officer. In December 1975 he returned to the Hotel (by then rebuilt to its former glory) to unveil a memorial plaque.

The wars of the first half of the 20th century brought many deaths among Torbay's young men and women. The Rolls of Honour record hundreds of names. Amongst the World War Two names is one from the Special Operations Executive who served behind enemy lines. Their dangerous work included the co-ordination of Resistance fighters with the Allied forces. Muriel Byck from Torquay died in May 1944 soon after being parachuted into France.

The period from 1950 to 2002 has added just five names, including one killed in Korea and another in the Falkands conflict.

The Hollywood that never was

TORBAY had a brief encounter with the cinema industry. In May 1919 an article appeared in the *Torquay Directory* headed 'Torquay – Los Angeles of England. Future centre of British film production'. The editor eulogised: 'It is not so much the strong sunshine and the clouds and the reflection and glare off the water. There was a remarkable variety of scenery – sea, the white roads, the red cliffs, the moors and the sylvan scenes without end'. It was reported also that the movies recently filmed in Torquay were *Beau Brocade*,

Nelson and *The Rocks of Valpre* ('shot' on the rocks at Corbyn beach and elsewhere). It was an innovative period for the industry in general. Those early films are among those preserved in the National Film Archive. At this time there was also an abortive attempt to set up a film studio in Paignton. In September 1919 the prospectus of Torquay and Paignton Photo-Play Productions was issued. It was intended that the Public Hall (now the Palace Theatre) should be bought, together with the island site across the road (now the Public Gardens). One

It may be hard to believe now, but one of the early film ventures mooted for Torbay was a company at Paignton headquartered on the Palace Avenue Public Hall and the island site opposite which became the gardens – seen here early in the last century. The Public Hall, now the Palace Theatre, is on the left.

Rock Walk in Torquay was a location for a 1920 film which needed a jungle setting.

most modern and up-to-date studios in England'. There were two studios, dark and light; each had the latest equipment and practically any motion picture could be completed within the grounds of the studios. The first of these was completed in May 1920. It was an adaptation of *Unrest* by Warwick Deeping. The jungle scenes were filmed in Rock Walk on the sea front. The producer explained that 'the paths are covered with artificial jungle grass, a human baboon clings to the branches of an old ash tree and sailors climb over the steep slopes as if they have landed on a tropical island'. It cost £6,000 to make. Later *Where the Rainbow Ends*, the film of the play (which had been running in London and elsewhere for several years) was filmed at Watcombe. Production ceased soon afterwards.

In December 1920 Stoll Theatres Ltd announced that three major productions would be filmed in Torquay. Top director Maurice Elvey arrived with 45 actors to make *The Amateur Gentleman* by Jeffrey Farnol. Scenes were shot at Babbacombe, Anstey's Cove and in St Marychurch. There was also a horse race scene with 43 horses in action; this was run on the Racecourse (now the Golf Course at Petitor). Later, in 1924, Stoll was again in Torquay to make Emmeline Morrison's *The Sins Ye Do*. Scenes were shot on Thatcher Rock, on Corbyn Beach and elsewhere.

In March 1925 Watcombe Hall came on the market when it was said to be 'equipped with a film-making studio... costing thousands of pounds... The studio is of latticed girders on a concrete and wood inlaid floor, one half being glazed for daylight

of the promoters was Mr J. Bamberger of Salt Lake City, Utah. The intention was that 'the Productions will be supervised by American Producers and will be taken by American Camera-men... The general policy of this Company will be to produce pictures of English life with essentially British atmosphere and British artistes. Clean pictures for clean-minded people is the Company's motto and slogan'. However, for all its apparently good intentions no more was heard of the company and it is not known if any Torbay people took advantage of the offer to buy shares.

It was in 1919 also that film studios were built in Torquay. Cairn's Torquay Film Company was formed and was located at Watcombe Hall. Cairn's decided to build studios (at a cost of £40,000) and rent them out on a contract basis. When the construction was nearly finished a brochure was sent out to potential users which offered 'the finest,

ABRIDGED PROSPECTUS.

A Copy of this Prospectus has been filed with the Registrar of Joint Stock Companies.
No part of this Issue has been underwritten.
No part of the proceeds of this Issue is to be applied for Capital purposes outside the United Kingdom, or to replace money which has been so applied.

TORQUAY & PAIGNTON PHOTO PLAY PRODUCTIONS, LIMITED
(Incorporated under the Companies Acts 1908 to 1917).

Capital - - £100,000.
DIVIDED INTO
60,000 10% Participating **Preference** Shares of £1 Each
AND
40,000 Ordinary Shares of £1 Each.

The Participating Preference Shares confer on the holders thereof the right out of the profits of each year which it shall be determined to distribute to receive a fixed Preferential Dividend for such year at the rate of 10 per cent. on the amount for the time being paid up on such shares and to one half of the remaining nett profits or other assets of the Company available for dividend which it shall from time to time be determined to distribute. The Ordinary Shares confer on the holders thereof the right to the remaining half of such remaining nett profits. The Participating Preference Shares also confer the right in a winding up to the re-payment of the amount paid thereon in preference to the Ordinary Shares and to one half of the surplus assets remaining after re-payment of the paid up capital of the Company.

PRESENT ISSUE.
60,000 10% PARTICIPATING PREFERENCE SHARES
are now offered for subscription at par, and payable:—
2/6 on Application; 2/6 on Allotment; 5/- 30 Days after Allotment;
5/- 60 Days after Allotment; 5/- 90 Days after Allotment.

Board of Directors:
REGINALD JACOB REUBENSON, Managing Director, 13 Gerrard Street, W.C. 1 (Cinematograph Film Importer and Exporter).
MAJOR-GENERAL SIR NORMAN ROBERT STEWART, Bart., C.B., 18 Freeland Road, Ealing, W.5.
ANDREW GODCHAUX, 31 Hatton Gardens, E.C. (Diamond and Pearl Merchant).
Bankers: LONDON JOINT CITY AND MIDLAND BANK, LIMITED, (Leicester Square Branch), 8 New Coventry Street, W.1.
Solicitors: Messrs. AMERY-PARKES & CO., 18 Fleet Street, E.C. 4.
Auditors: Messrs. CHANTREY, CHANTREY & Co., 61 Lincoln Inn Fields, W.C.
Registered Offices and Secretary:
12 & 13 Atlantic House, Holborn Viaduct, E.C. 1, London.
HARRY ALLEN, F.C.I.S., Secretary.

PROSPECTUS —
The primary objects of the Company are:—
To establish a British moving picture manufacturing business on commercial lines:
To acquire the Freehold Premises and buildings at Paignton and to convert and equip the same as Production Studios in accordance with the designs and plans approved by the Directors of the Company under the advice and assistance of American experts:
To establish a Sales Organisation for the sale and distribution of the Company's and other productions.
The business of moving picture production in this country has, in the past, suffered from lack of public appreciation of its possibilities and of financial support. No serious attempt has been made to establish the business on commercial lines, as in America.
The British investor is at last becoming alive to the importance of picture production, which offers a sound and lucrative investment, and which, in the near future, will become an important national industry.
The experience and knowledge acquired in picture production, and the ever increasing demand and ready market, have made it possible, under the guidance of experts, to establish the business as a stable commercial undertaking, with the prospect of exceptional profits from the production of pictures which appeal to the popular fancy.
There is a growing and insistent demand, not only in this country, but in the British Colonies and Europe, and even in America itself, for British productions depicting phases of British life, socially, industrially and commercially, its characteristics and habits, its unrivalled

The prospectus published in the *Torquay Directory* in September 1919 which hoped to establish a motion picture industry. Also seen is the editorial mention of the same initiative.

succession.

TORQUAY AND PAIGNTON PHOTO PLAY PRODUCTIONS, LTD.

In another column will be found the prospectus of the above Company, who are issuing 60,000 10 per cent Participating Preference Shares at £1 each. This is the Company which purchased the Public Hall, Paignton, for the production of photo plays. John Robarts and Co., of 12 and 13 Atlantic House, Holburn Viaduct, London, have prepared an illustrated booklet, fully describing the business of the Torquay and Paignton Photoplay Productions Limited, and the large profits that are now being made in the Moving Picture Industry. They will be pleased to forward a copy of this publication to all who are interested, free of cost, upon request. A postal will bring you the complete information.

work, the other half for use by artificial light'. The Hall was sold to Mr J.P. Moore later but he made no attempt to resume film-making there. This appeared to be the end of the story because the quality of lenses used in ciné-photography had so improved that natural light was no longer essential. Film studios were being built in London, convenient both for stars and technicians.

Except for location filming by several companies in the 1930s there were no developments until after World War Two when, surprisingly, two attempts were made to re-establish the industry in Torbay. The old Watcombe Studio, after being a store for the furniture of bombed-out people, became in 1946 the location for the Torquay Studios, a company recently formed under the chairmanship of Mr C.W. Baschwitz. It was, he said, to be 'one of the principal outdoor film locations in England'. Equipment worth £100,000 was said to have been bought; however, there is no evidence that it had been. After giving approval there were doubts in the minds of many councillors as to whether this should be allowed and so a deputation from the Council visited Ealing Studios. They promptly rescinded the resolution in favour! The deputation also disapproved of the props they saw lying around 'such as farm carts loaded with stock, dead sheep and broken-down taxicabs and we were told that this sort of thing was bound to accumulate wherever there is a studio'. The structure remained unused for the next 30 years. After serving as a store for beach floats, it was finally pulled down in 1980.

The attempt to start film-making again at Paignton was not in the town centre but at Paignton Council's newly-acquired Oldway Mansion. In February 1948 it was reported that filming would start in May. *Dead Ground*, with an all-star cast directed by Lance Comfort (the managing director) would be the first film. However, just two months later there was criticism from visiting film directors who realised that the facilities they saw would never compare with modern studios elsewhere. They concluded that the project would be a failure – and it was. Nevertheless a great deal of work was carried out including the complete sound-proofing of the Rotunda. A special power-station with three diesel generators was put in; these annoyed the neighbours greatly. Production ended after only a few short pictures had been shot. When the interior was being inspected in 1994, the sound-proofing was still on the walls.

It is a little ironic that now, in 2003, West Country locations are being offered and are in great demand. The successful *Sense and Sensibility* was just one recent production. This was because of the 'clarity of the air, the small amount of exterior noise (like high-flying jets) and the good weather'.

The press we read and the television we watch

THE importance of newspapers in Torquay's recent history was told in the *Centenary History* published in 1992: 'At the beginning of this century, there were two weekly newspapers edited by men of stature and integrity. They were the *Torquay Directory* (which had commenced publishing in 1839), edited by Mr William Winget whilst at the *Torquay Times* (every Friday from 1865) Mr George H. Brierley controlled editorial policy. Winget attained his 80th birthday in January 1923. He was an outstanding journalist and continued to write articles recounting Torquay's past as the 'memories of an octogenarian'.

In the 1980s the *Herald Express* began to produce 'Torbay and South Devon Bygones' supplements in tabloid form. Among the early productions were 'Royal Devon' in 1983 and 'Transport Bygones' two years later. Perhaps the most important of the 1990s was 'The Agatha Bygones: the life and times of Agatha Christie' in November 1990. This was printed on good-quality paper and cost just 50p. 'Our War: memories of the Home Front in South Devon' was a wonderful record in 1989 in words and pictures (many seen in print for the first time) of World War Two. This too cost just 50p. There was some disappointment among readers when the printing of the *Herald Express* was moved to Plymouth and, shortly afterwards, everything was printed on the high-speed, high-quality presses of

The front page of the first *Herald Express* on 13 July 1925 and, below, the masthead as it had become in 1939. The word 'Torbay' had already disappeared and despite the paper losing the '&' part of its title in the war years it is still referred to as the *Herald and Express* by older people.

Associated Newspapers. All the later 'Bygones', particularly those in December 1997 (that issue reproduced Stephen Bretton's fine century-old hand-coloured glass slides) and the 'Millennium Story' among others have full-colour pictures of a standard of which earlier editors could only have dreamed.

Frequent references have been made to stories that appeared in the *Torquay Times*, owned at one time by Mr W.J. MacKenzie, but later owned and edited by Mr George Lidstone who arrived in the

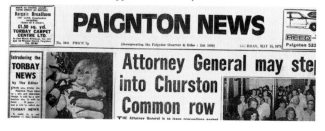

First issue of the *Paignton News* dated 24 September 1932 and the last issue on 15 May 1976 – a front page panel informed readers that from the following week it would appear as the *Torbay News*.

1930s and continued in charge for many years (until the paper was bought by another group in 1966). The *Torquay Directory* had the sub-title *and South Devon Journal*. This replaced the original masthead in 1949 and the paper continued to be published as a tabloid until the 1960s.

In the last two decades a new phenomenon has appeared on the scene, the free newspaper. It reached Torquay when the *Weekender* started publication and is now a companion paper to the *Herald Express*.

The Higgs family recorded news and other stories for over half a century in the *Paignton Observer*. Many fascinating news items were written by Gilbert Day, for many years the *Observer's* only reporter. In one story he describes the burial of Boris Heroys 'Major General, Russian Imperial Army, Soldier and Artist'. At the time of his death in 1942 he was living

The *Paignton Observer* of 10 September 1942 with a wartime story of bombing fatalities – though the censorship of the day prevented any mention of the actual locality of the raid. Below is the penultimate issue of the *Observer* on 23 August 1962 – after the following week's issue the paper was taken over by the *Paignton News*.

in Colin Road, Paignton. Earlier he had enjoyed a distinguished military career having served in the Russian Imperial Army Foot Guards. The service at Collaton St Mary Church was conducted by Father Michael of the Orthodox Church in London and was delivered according to its ritual. Throughout the service 'each mourner carried a lighted candle; the body was in full military uniform and it was only after the service that the coffin was closed'. During World War two Gilbert Day took over the role of editor as well – many of its wartime stories came from his pen. In the immediate post-war period when newsprint was scarce and its quality poor, the *Observer* took the opportunity to publish, in instalments, Charles Patterson's *Book of Paignton*. This subsequently was published in bound form using the original hand-set type and was for many years the only well-researched history of the town.

The *Brixham Western Guardian* (1902 to 1968) had just a page or so of local stories but its files are one of the few sources of Brixham's history over the period. Cuttings taken from it by the Council for official records show what life in the town in the war years. One such cutting, of 1940, tells us: 'Sufficient fabric window netting to cover the window area in one room or passage will be issued free to eligible persons'. Later in 1941: 'All male persons between the ages of 16 and 60 residing in Brixham must register for Civil Defence duties'. This was followed by a notice explaining the role of the Fire Guard, the requirement being 48 hours of duty in each period of four weeks. Finally, in December that year, there was an appeal for residents to take custody of sandbags 'rather than leaving them beside lamp posts'. Just a year later, the people were being urged to save all fuel and keep up stocks. They were told that purchases must not exceed 12cwt. 1942 was also the year when all unnecessary railings were requisitioned. In May 1943 the British Restaurant opened in Rea Barn Road, another at Bolton Cross becoming available to priority ticket-holders only. The improving war situation was shown by the notice in August 1944 when unwanted Morrison shelters were to be collected by the Council. These were sent to London as the 'buzz-bombs' and rockets had started to fall on the capital.

Because of their easy access on microfilm in local libraries, most of the stories told here have been

Torquay's weekly paper of record for many generations was the *Torquay Times*, seen here on 8 April 1949. The alternative to the cliff railway at Babbacombe involved a lift between the beach and the clifftop, while the picture shows the Town Hall being floodlit for the first time since wartime restrictions on the use of electricity. The *Torquay Times* ceased publication in 1976.

taken from the *Herald Express, Torquay Times* and *Torquay Directory*. However, other titles have appeared on the news-stands; these include the *Brixham Chronicle* and the *Paignton News*. The *News* was started in 1932 by the Torquay Times Group and remained in existence for 30 years.

A valuable resource not covered in detail here is the *Western Morning News* which dates from 1860 and has been covering South Devon stories ever since. Early issues can be seen only at the British Library.

Torbay receives good radio and television signals from both local and more distant transmitters. North Hessary Tor on Dartmoor transmits strong radio signals on all BBC channels, including Radio Devon (which replaced the South West Regional Programme in 1983). There is a medium-wave station at Preston. Commercial radio began when Devonair began broadcasting in April 1981. It now operates on AM and FM as Gemini Radio.

When Queen Elizabeth II was crowned in 1953 the only television transmitter serving the south-west was at Wenvoe in South Wales. The small number of people who were able to view the event had to watch the misty black-and-white pictures on the very small screens of those early sets. The BBC's

transmitter at North Hessary Tor served Torbay and South Devon, and independent television, which took to the air in 1955, erected their own transmitter at Stockland Hill in East Devon. Both transmitted on the 405-lines standard. Aerials facing in the two directions were required; in some parts of Torbay reception was none too clear on one, or even both of the television channels then available. When the new transmitter opened at Beacon Hill in 1972, it operated on the 625-lines system. This provided much better picture quality but there were still problems with reception levels in low-lying parts of the area.

Early in the early 1990s the situation was improved greatly when small relay stations were set up around Torbay. The original commercial Westward Television was replaced with Television South West and later still by Westcountry. This became part of the Carlton Group and now transmits as Carlton Westcountry. As we enter the 21st century digital television and broadband are becoming familiar terms. Digital television signals are now broadcast from Beacon Hill (in addition to analogue signals) and the arrival of cable television in some parts of the area mean that state-of-the-art communications are on their way.

Torbay people

A DECADE or so ago the Torbay Civic Society began its Blue Plaque programme to honour townspeople who had made major contributions to Torbay's life and institutions. The plaques record places and buildings throughout Torbay of historic importance. For each plaque a pamphlet has been published outlining the reason each subject has been chosen. Other plaques recognise buildings with connections to such eminent people as writers Charles Kingsley, who lived at Livermead House in Torquay, and Elizabeth Barrett Browning who moved to Torquay in 1838 for the benefit of her health.

Indeed, the entire Torbay area is littered with connections to people of note, both local and those who made their homes there. Though it would be quite impossible to list all of Torbay's famous sons and daughters, what follows is a brief outline of the lives and contributions of some of them.

AGATHA CHRISTIE was born Agatha Mary Clarissa Miller in September 1890 at Ashfield in Barton Road, Torquay (a house now replaced by modern flats). Her father was American and her mother English. She spent her formative years as 'a young lady of quality'.

The family were well-off thanks to her father's thriving New York business. On Christmas Eve 1914 she married Archibald Christie, a pilot in the Royal Flying Corps. She spent many years as a dispensary assistant which stood her in good stead during a writing career in which she became arguably the best-known mystery writer in the English Language.

The young Agatha Miller pictured in the garden at Ashfield.

After a second marriage in 1930 to Sir Max Mallowan, an archaeologist, the couple continued to use the family home until they bought Greenway House from Sir Arthur Goodson for £6,000. Dame Agatha Christie, as she became in 1971, died in 1976 at Wallingford in Oxfordshire. Her Torquay home had, however, remained under family ownership and in March 2000 Greenway passed into the ownership of the National Trust.

More than 2 billion copies of her books have been published, and her work, which has been translated into more than 40 languages, is outsold only by the Bible and William Shakespeare.

The Agatha Christie legacy lives on in Torbay. In early 1997 the 'Christie Mile' was launched in Torquay. The *Herald Express* explained that plaques had been put up at the Yacht Club, the Museum, the Tourist Centre, the Pavilion and other locations with Agatha Christie connections. The walk starts at the Imperial (the Majestic hotel of her novels) and ends at the Grand Hotel (where the Christies spent their honeymoon).

Agatha Christie was not Torbay's only literary star. ELIZABETH GOUDGE, a shy and reclusive novelist, moved to Providence Cottage in Marldon in 1939. The district subsequently figured widely in her writing. *Moonacre Manor* was inspired by Compton Castle; *Gentian Hill, Green Dolphin Country* and her story for children *Smokey House* all had Marldon village scenes written in to them. *Gentian Hill* achieved wide circulation in the United States in a book-club edition and was a clever retelling of a 19th century folk-legend of Torquay.

FLORA THOMPSON, too, was a writer with local connections. She was born Flora Jane Timms at Juniper Hill near Brackly in December 1876. Her link with South Devon began when her husband John became postmaster at Dartmouth in 1928. The family lived at the Outlook in Above Town for 12 years and it was here that she completed *Lark Rise*, published in 1939, which was based on her childhood experiences. In 1940 John retired from the Post Office and they moved to Lauriston, off New Road in Brixham. It was not long after moving there that her youngest son, Peter, was lost whilst in the Merchant Navy, his ship being torpedoed in mid-Atlantic. Her classics on country life were completed after his death. The first was *Candleford*

Green, 'several of the passages (being) written with the bombs falling' and when she was in the indoor Morrison shelter. *Still Glides the Stream* was completed only a few weeks before she died on 21 May 1947, 'suddenly and alone in her room'. Flora is buried in Longcross Cemetery in Dartmouth, the memorial stone being shaped like an open book. One half has the inscription to her loved son, who has no grave. It is inscribed: 'Peter Redmond lost at sea Sept. 6th 1941'.

HENRY FRANCIS LYTE, minister and hymn-writer, although born in Scotland, had strong local connections. The writer of many of the nation's favourite hymns, he was vicar of All Saints' in Brixham. Among his best-known works are *Abide With Me*, and *Praise My Soul, the King of Heaven*. Lyte died in Nice in 1847.

OLIVER HEAVISIDE, mathematician, physicist and eccentric, was a genius and was recognised as such during his lifetime. On 5 March 1896 'in consideration of his work in connexion with the theory of electricity' he was granted a government pension of £120 per annum. This was later increased by £100 per annum. In 1908 he moved to Homefield

Oliver Heaviside, after whom the 'Heaviside Layer' in the ionosphere was named. After further scientific work, this is now known as the 'Kennelly-Heaviside Layer'.

in Lower Warberry Road, Torquay (now the Elmarino Holiday Flats, outside which a plaque was erected in the 1970s), where his lifestyle was strange in the extreme. Although a man of genius, he had little commonsense. Towards the end of his life he was desperately short of money and was, according to one report, without gas and heat from August 1921 to October 1925. His eccentricities included, it is believed, papering the walls with unpaid gas bills and decorating the trees in his garden with rate demands. Heaviside died in a nursing home in February 1925 and was buried in Paignton cemetery.

ERNEST BROWN, politician, was Torquay-born, his father a coxswain of the Torquay lifeboat. Ernest had a long career in Parliament serving under Stanley Baldwin. He had a number of important posts in World War Two including Minister of Labour (1935–40); Minister of Health (1941–3) and Chancellor of the Duchy of Lancaster (1943–5). Brown was a Baptist all his life and proudly acted as a lay preacher whenever possible.

HERBERT WHITLEY'S fascination with animals began during childhood when his mother gave him a pair of canaries. He went on to breed finches,

Herbert Whitley, a very private man of whom very few photographs survive, was the founder of Paignton Zoo.

rabbits and poultry and, in 1904 when the Whitleys leased Primley House from the Belfield family (thus ending the Belfields' long connection with Paignton), Herbert began collecting and breeding domestic and rare breeds. Soon his collection expanded to include more exotic species and, after World War One, he looked to founding his own business. In 1923 what would eventually become Paignton Zoo and Environmental Park opened to the public to great acclaim. Whitley's legacy continues, providing entertainment and education to a further generation of Torbay's residents and visitors.

JAMES HUTCHINSON VC of the 2nd/5th Lancashire Fusiliers was Torbay's only holder of the Victoria Cross, winning his medal on 20 June 1916 whilst leading a bombing party after his officer-in-charge had been shot. In the same raid his brother and 20 other men were killed. Hutchinson survived the war, joining up again in 1939. He was fit enough to return to Flanders for the 50th Anniversary of the battle.

Several prominent families moved into Torbay from abroad. Isaac Singer and his wife, Isabella Eugenie Boyer, moved to Torbay from France where Isabella had been the model for the Statue of Liberty. Singer had made his fortune in the United States where, while working as a labourer, he had invented the first mechanical excavator. But it was his development and marketing of the sewing machine that ensured that the name of Singer would endure. Isaac and Isabella had six children (of the 24 Isaac is said to have fathered in and out of wedlock.) They were: Adam, Winnaretta, Paris, Washington, Isabelle Blanche and Franklin.

ADAM MORTIMER SINGER was the eldest of these; and by 1920 after being knighted,when he lived at Astra House Warren Road in Torquay, he appears to have dropped his first name becoming Sir Mortimer Singer. Whilst in Egypt in 1910 he had been badly injured falling out of an aeroplane but must have made a good recovery. This episode clearly did not deter him from flying because, in May 1914, 'Mr and Mrs Mortimer Singer left London at 12.23 in the balloon *Planet*. They landed at Launceston 200 miles away; it was the first balloon voyage from London to Cornwall'. Singer was a keen yachtsman and after owning the yacht *Triad* for a time, started racing in a 12-metre yacht

Paris Singer, the man who transformed Oldway Mansion into the Versailles style we see today.

Winnaretta Singer painted in her younger years.

called *Lulworth*. Ned Heard, a 'lower-deck' man, became his skipper; such an action was unheard of among the other gentlemen-yachtsmen of his day. When sailing Sopwith's *Endeavour I* back from the USA following her unsuccessful attempt on the Americas Cup, the tow-rope parted and the yacht was feared lost. Indeed *Endeavour* was posted

missing at Lloyds. However, Singer finally brought the vessel safely to port. The J-class yacht *Astra* raced for some years under his ownership. Sir Mortimer died on 24 June 1929; the service and funeral took place soon after and he was interred in the family vault in Torquay Cemetery.

PARIS EUGENE SINGER, was named after the place of his birth, although he sometimes used his second name. He was born in November 1868 and was Isaac and Isabella's third child. After he grew up he had houses in London and Paris and built an opulent retreat on the French Riviera where he maintained a yacht with a crew of 50. He studied architecture in Paris where he obtained a degree. It stood him good stead when in 1893 he took over the Oldway estate from his father's trustees and, as governing director of the Paignton and District Development Co, developed much of Preston (he had also bought the Redcliffe estate in 1893), Oldway and Barcombe. Paris was keenly interesting in motoring (being at one time Honorary Secretary of the AA) and was one of the first people in the West Country to see the possibilities of the aeroplane as a means of transport – he had a hangar built on Preston Green. Between 1904 and 1907 he

Winnaretta Singer photographed in later life as the Princesse de Polignac, patron of the arts.

This rare picture showing the original front of Oldway Mansion with its elaborate conservatory-like structures, is reputed to show Paris Singer in the car ascending the ramp which led to the entrance hall on the first floor. It was Paris, Isaac Singer's third son by Isabella Boyer, who rebuilt Oldway in the style of the Palace of Versailles, near Paris. The picture below shows work in progress.

Mortimer Singer, yachtsman.

undertook the major task of remodelling Oldway with the help of his architect, Mr J.H. Cooper. The grounds were laid out by Achille Duchene (who also designed Blenheim Palace's water garden). At the time of his death in June 1932 he had four sons (including Cecil, who lived at Occombe) and a daughter (who became Lady Leeds). Paris, too, was buried in the Singer vault.

His liaison with Isadora Duncan (whom he met in 1909 after he had separated from his wife) has been well documented. Although their trial marriage at Oldway failed, she remained his mistress for a further seven years. The *Times*, in April 1913, reports the death of their son Patrick, along with his half-sister Deirdre and their English nanny: 'The car... left Mme Duncan's house in the Rue Chauveau at 3.20pm in order to take the children for a drive to Versailles. It had only gone a few hundred yards when the driver had to pull up suddenly to avoid a taxi-cab. Masserand (her chauffeur) had to leave his seat to turn the crank before the car could be restarted. In all probability he had not properly adjusted the speed lever, since before he could

remount the car it started of itself and proceeded at a rapid rate across the Boulevard Bourdon... down the grassy bank of the Seine and from whence it plunged into the river'. Firemen were called and a large motor-boat requisitioned but it was an hour and a half before the car could be hauled ashore. There were no survivors. Isadora herself died in 1927 when one of her trademark flowing scarves became entangled in the wheel of the Bugatti in which she was travelling and broke her neck. Another son of Isaac and Isabella was WASHING-TON MERRITT SINGER, who was living at Benet Wood in the Warberries when he died in February 1934. When first married he lived at Steartfield House which he enlarged (this later became the Paignton Palace Hotel). After inheriting $1 million from his father, he decided to go ranching in the American West but was discouraged by one of his brothers; he took up hunting instead and started to breed horses. His stables were at the junction of Manor Road and Old Torquay Road. One of his horses, Challacombe, won the St Leger in 1905. The Merritt Flats for working people, with frontages on the Totnes Road, were one of his acts of charity.

DAME VIOLET WILLS, the philanthropist, was the daughter of Sir Edward Payson Wills of Bristol, a

One of Torbay's major benefactors in the 20th century was Ella Rowcroft, who gave money to enable a new Torbay Hospital to be built near Lawes Bridge in the late 1920s. One of her Torquay homes, Rainbow (below), became part of the Rowcroft Hospice in 1997, the hospice having originated in the adjacent Pilmuir, her earlier home which she had given to the hospital and which became the hospice in 1982.

member of the tobacco family. She lived in both Torquay and Paignton, but her main residence was at Bel Alp in Haytor Vale. This house had its own air-raid shelter as well as a private chapel and the garage had room for several Rolls-Royces. Her Anglican faith was strong and she welcomed many local churchmen to her home; she also offered holidays to them and to their wives. Tranquillity in St Luke's Road was given and dedicated by Dame Violet in 1924 as a home of rest 'in memory of those clergy

who have faithfully preached the Word of God and for the rest and refreshment of those striving to do the same'. Some of the furniture chosen by Dame Violet was still there in 1990 and she also presented an ambulance for use in World War Two. Among other things, she was an officer of the Order of St John of Jerusalem. She died in 1964 aged 97.

Dame Violet's sister, MRS ELLA ROWCROFT, shared her philanthropic nature. Mrs Rowcroft gave £100,000 towards the building of the new hospital (which was completed in 1928) and a further £6,000 as an endowment fund for a chaplain there providing that 'they must be Christian Churchmen… free from the questionable modernist teachings of the Anglo-Catholic and RC Churches'. Dame Violet gave the same establishment £6,500 for a Radio Therapy Department and the sisters' many gifts to the hospital are commemorated in their names being given to hospital wards.

Mrs Rowcroft was already a widow when she moved from Paignton to Pilmuir – a large house rebuilt by a Mr Backhouse. She lived there from 1920 to 1938, when she moved to the newly-built Rainbow next door. It was said to be one of the last modern mansions to be built in the county before World War Two. In 1937 Mrs Rowcroft gave Pilmuir to the Hospital as a convalescent home provided that 'no card playing, betting or gambling, dancing or theatricals shall be permitted in the Home'. A Trust was formed a few months later and the Rowcroft Convalescent Home took its first patients, ladies only, in April 1939. Many recuperated there until 1981, when it closed through lack of funds. Mainly due to the efforts of Torquay Lions Club the former home became Rowcroft Hospice and was opened officially by David Dimbleby in July 1982. The 1990s saw an ambitious extension scheme culminating in the purchase of Rainbow in December 1997. The last five years have seen even more improvements and developments, all funded with massive help from the people of Torbay. The Wills Trust is still active and continues to support 'good causes'.

Ironically, given the origins of their wealth, neither sister would not allow smoking anywhere in or outside their homes.

A particular feature of the 20th century was the departure of the influential landed families from the social scene. Successive generations had lived in their great houses for hundreds of years – but World War One had come and a generation of men too young to have started families and thus produce heirs had been diminished.

The CARYS, who had been lords of the manor of Cockington since the 14th century, moved 'next door' when, in 1662, they bought Torre Abbey and part of Tormohun for £800. Successive generations of the family, passing the manor from father to son, continued to live there for the next 300 years. Colonel Lucius and Mrs Cary came back in July 1907 to live at Torre Abbey. It was the return of the lord of the manor in every sense. To celebrate his homecoming, 500 leaseholders and tenants contributed to a testimonial, the main gifts being a massive silver salver and a silver jardinière, both embellished with the Cary arms. When Henry Cary, the only son of Lucius and his first wife, died in the Boer War, no direct heir to the estate existed, and the nearest relative was his cousin, Sulyarde Cary. There was, however, a problem with a cousin inheriting as an 'entail' intended to guarantee continued family ownership and which dated back to medieval times, had first to be broken. This process was completed in 1912 and the new heir-in-law was now Sulyarde's son, Lancelot. At the outbreak of World War One Lancelot joined the 9th Battalion of the Devonshire Regiment but was killed in action at the Battle of the Somme on 20 July 1916. Because of delays in settling Colonel Lucius's affairs, Lancelot had only received his inheritance on 1 July. He had been lord of the manor of Torre Abbey for barely three weeks. The very young casualty had died unmarried and without producing a direct male heir. In turn Lancelot had willed the estate to Captain Lionel

Henry St Croix Coxon, the son of a sister of Colonel Cary. A condition of the inheritance was that Captain Coxon could do so only if and when he assume the family name. His son was also required to do the same. Captain Lionel Cary (formerly Coxon) died in May 1929. His obituary noted: 'Unhappily extremely heavy death duties meant that he had never achieved his dearest wish of living at Torre Abbey'. It was soon after this death that the Mansion House and adjacent lands were sold for £40,000 to the Borough of Torquay.

The MALLOCK FAMILY had lived for nearly 300 years at Cockington Court as lords of the manor. Charles Henry Mallock was the last of his family to live permanently at Cockington Court. After his father's death he had returned to a spectacular homecoming – there was a long procession and a firework display. The birth of his son and heir, Richard Herbert Mallock, took place soon after that return. Charles Mallock rejoined the Army at the outbreak of World War One, serving with distinction on the Western Front; sadly, he died in 1917 after inhaling mustard gas. When his father died, Richard was only nine years old. He returned to Cockington in November 1928 with his stepfather just in time for his coming of age and immediately brought about changes that made him unpopular with the locals. For many years the estate church had been popular and freely available for the use of all. However, the new arrivals replaced the old dilapidated gate with a massive new one, a lock was fitted and all access forbidden (except to parishioners when attending church). Although peace was later restored, it was not long before Cockington Court and its 223 acres passed into public ownership. It had cost just £30,000.

Headlines from the last half-century

Food rationing and a healthy diet

WITHIN days of the declaration of war in 1939, plans were announced for rationing meat and petrol. The books issued for the latter, initially, covered a period of two months but did not say how much each coupon would be worth. Coal and coke rationing was added to the list of rationed goods before long. Among the duties of the Food (Defence Plan) Department, which had its HQ in Oxford, was one to control the supply of fish and to ensure that the Fish Friers' Associations had supplies for the country's fish and chips. As the months and years progressed the range of rationed goods was expanded, and the individual weekly allowance was reduced again and again. Millions of Points Coupon Books were issued. These were, of course, more usually known as the Ration Book. Some of the notes on them seem draconian today: 'You must always have your book with you

This picture postcard shows what was called the 'Brixham Baptist Sunday School Demonstration' of 1907, with the procession passing the King William statue.

A fine picture from 1937 of the Royal Yacht *Victoria and Albert* in Tor Bay; on board were George VI and Queen Elizabeth, apparently with the two young princesses (if this statement was true this presumably represents our present monarch's first visit to Torbay). The royal visitors were en route to Dartmouth for an inspection at the Britannia Royal Naval College. Note the speedboat *Miss Torbay 1* 'buzzing' the royal vessel. The *Victoria and Albert* was the third Royal Yacht of that name and the 83rd in a line stretching back to Charles II in 1660. This third *V & A* was reckoned to be the largest Royal Yacht in the world at 4,700 tons, with a crew of 367. She had been launched in 1899 for Queen Victoria, who in fact never sailed in her, and ultimately became a depot ship at Portsmouth; she was broken up at Faslane in 1955. In 1938 the Admiralty began to consider building her replacement and *Britannia*, the last of our Royal Yachts, was launched in 1953. She was decommissioned in 1997 and is now a charitable trust in Scotland. There was often more than one 'Royal Yacht' at the same time and a *Britannia* sailing yacht was built in 1893 for the Prince of Wales, later Edward VII. She was later inherited by George V and was well known in competitive sailing events – it is this *Britannia* that is pictured in the chapter 'All At Sea'. George V ruled that after his death she was to be scuttled at sea and this was accomplished off the Isle of Wight in 1936.

when you use them and the retailer will cut them out. You must not cut them out yourself… You will be told from time to time for what foods they are needed'. Everyone was required to register, and was given a National Registration Number. Even as the war came to a close, there was a public notice in all the papers: 'How to get your New Ration Book at the Electricity Show Room, Castle Circus, Monday, 28 May 1945, 9.30am-6.00pm'.

Although VE Day brought bonfires, parades and street parties, residents emphasised that the spreads were only possible because of co-operative efforts among neighbours. It was clear that rationing would not end with the peace. In fact, it was to continue well into peacetime so that those too young to remember the war itself remember only too well the years of shortages that followed.

Organisations across the world, but particularly in the British Empire and the United States, had begun to send food parcels to beleaguered Britain. These care packages continued to arrive well after hostilities ended in 1945. In July 1947 a brief news item reported the arrival of 11lb of ham-loaf, jam, honey, cheese, Christmas pudding, beef suet and dried milk as a gift to the people of Torquay from members of the Torquay Golf Club, Australia.

Prisoners-of-war at work

Although our own prisoners-of-war began arriving home almost as soon as hostilities ceased, Germans and Italians in Britain remained as labourers for some time after the war ended. Both nationalities were in Torbay following their capture in various theatres of operation. The Prudential huts at Shiphay were used to house Italians. Here they were kept behind high fences through which they would push wood-carvings to any children passing by. Early in 1947 German prisoners-of-war were employed to lay gas mains in Hartop Road and elsewhere. They made and sold rope slippers to local people to obtain small amounts of English currency. Later in the year the Germans who were billeted locally were given permission to visit cafes and enter cinemas. However, few took advantage of this as they had little money to spare after they had bought their cigarettes.

Torbay as an international and national conference venue

The Olympic yachting events in 1948 had put Torbay on the world map. As a result several conferences of international importance were staged there. In the months prior to the arrival of the GATT (General Agreement on Tariffs and Trade) Conference in 1950, the streets were opened up for the laying of five miles of cables with a capacity for nearly 1,000 telephone lines. Delegates began to arrive on 27 September, among them Harold Wilson – then in his mid-30s – at that time President of the Board of Trade and leader of the British delegation.

Their arrival prompted the headline: 'Secret Trade Lists at Torquay. Closely guarded against Disruptive Practices'. Plenary Sessions were held in the Cooling Lounge at the Marine Spa. Headquarters were at the Princes Hotel on Park Hill. Thirty former policemen, in special uniforms, maintained a constant watch and MI5 were said to have carefully vetted even the most humble employees. The GPO brought in 23 girl telephonists, eight of them linguists. They manned the switchboard 24 hours a day. There was a request early on for a rise in salary as it was claimed that the girls were having to pay £3 a week for bed, breakfast and evening meal. They were subsequently given an average of 25s a week towards the living expenses: not generous even then. The Torquay Protocol, as the negotiated document was named, was finally signed on 21 April 1951 although some 'delegates viewed with apprehension that 18-inch pile of documents (festooned with blue ribbons) which lay on the table of the Cooling Lounge'. Each delegate planted a lime tree (there were 42 in all) called at the time Cockington's Unter den Lindens. Most have survived, and, with their younger replacements, today form the elegant avenue between Higher Lodge and Cockington Court.

In September 1961, another important gathering was held in Torquay. This was the European Postal and Telecommunications Associations group, daily sessions being held at Torre Abbey and elsewhere. It was an early example of how the world was learning to deal with the large number of representatives speaking a multitude of languages. On this occasion sound-proof booths were set up for each of the official languages and specialists were brought in (who provided the instant and simultaneous translations of the discussions that could be heard through the special headsets provided). The occasion warranted the issue of special postage stamps. These were for twopence, fourpence and tenpence (all in 'old money'). These modest amounts show the scale of price-inflation over the 40 years since. Even in the 1960s Torquay could not offer a large conference hall, but many important bodies sent representatives with delegates numbering several thousands.

When the British Medical Association was in the town, with a royal visit from HRH the Duke of

One of Torquay's most famous fires was the blaze in 1939 at the Strand department store of Williams and Cox.

A fine view of a Victory tea party in 1945, marking the end of the war. This one was of the old Strand ward and was held close to the Alpine Inn on the Braddons hillsides.

One of the international gatherings which, like the Yachting Olympics in 1948, helped to put Torbay on the map was the GATT (General Agreement on Tariffs and Trade) Conference in 1950. Seen here are AA men (note the uniform) putting out direction signs; a seating plan at the Marine Spa; and one of the many tree plantings at Cockington to mark the conference.

Edinburgh in June 1962, members were reminded of earlier visits, the first in 1860 (when Torquay's Dr Radclyffe Hall presided) and again in 1906 when the BMA was in Devon and a large number spent the day in Torbay. Other annual conferences at that time included the Library Association (their first visit was in 1959) and the Royal Society for the Prevention of Accidents in 1964.

A popular annual event was the Torquay International Gastronomic Festival. Mr R. Paul of the Grand Hotel was the principal instigator and the event was held there in the 1950s and 1960s – and revived at other venues in the 1970s. It had begun in 1949 as a cocktail competition and culinary display, and subsequently grew from this modest beginning. It did much to bring cooks young and old to Torbay.

The harbourside and Beacon Hill

Coral Island opened on Beacon Hill in June 1977. Leased out by the Torbay Council, it failed to be profitable to the operator and was closed down in September 1988. For over 10 years the complex lay idle and unused.

Various schemes were proposed, from conversion to a religious centre, to the site becoming a fish restaurant; all failed to materialise. In September 2000 a new plan was proposed. Known as the Waterfront Project, the redevelopment of the area would include an exciting new attraction. 'Living Coasts' was announced to be a 'world-class aquatic and animal visitor attraction focussing on the conservation of coastal and marine life around the

Prince Philip lends a hand with the window at the Queen makes an appearance at Torquay Town Hall during her visit in May 1956. A crowd estimated at 10,000 gathered at Castle Circus and the Queen made three appearances at the window. The Queen is also seen at Torre Abbey, escorted by the then Mayor of Torquay, Kenneth R. Bryant, with the Duke of Edinburgh walking with the Lord Lieutenant of Devon, the Earl Fortsecue. Note that in the background, the Mayor's Officer and Mace Bearer, Bill Baxter, carries the mace reversed (upside down) in deference to the Sovereign's presence.

Pictured here on the campaign trail during a 1960s general election is Sir Frederic Bennett, Torbay's once long-serving Conservative MP. It is not clear why he and Lady Bennett were pictured at this location at Preston but it is probably something to do with the then controversy surrounding a new one-way traffic system – one can see the temporary kerbs directing Paignton-bound traffic to the left into Seaway Lane.

globe'. Under the control of Paignton Zoo, Whitbread and the local authority the development would also introduce many inter-connected businesses and services, including a purpose-built family pub to the area. Subsequently the waterproofing of the Inner Harbour was completed and a cill (bitterly opposed by many)

built between the Fish and Eastern Quays, an ornamental over-bridge being erected over it. Failure to obtain Lottery funding was reported in the *Herald Express,* but in spite of this the whole scheme went ahead in mid-2002. At that time the estimated cost was £21 million. The bridge was opened in May 2003.

Torquay gained international fame and publicity from 1964 with its Gastronomic Festivals, centred on the Torquay Technical College's catering department and the Imperial Hotel. One leading light of the festivals was the Imperial's general manager Michael Chapman, seen here holding some papers as he escorted his principal guest and official opener, Lady Salisbury (later to become Raine, Countess of Spencer and mother of the late Princess Diana) in 1968.

The latest – and largest – improvement

When South West Water Services Ltd was formed in 1989, it promised a 'Clean Sweep' programme for Torbay as soon as possible. The problems of floating sewage would be gone forever. The company put two options before the residents; one for a major sewerage works to be built in a deep quarry at Brokenbury near Churston, the other for a plant at Sharkham serviced by a new road winding from Hillhead to the coast. Eventually the former site was chosen and, in February 1998, a model of the proposed building was produced, together with a detailed description of the major works that would have to be carried out. To allay the many criticisms and concerns of environmental damage, a major tree-planting scheme was promised once the work was completed. A French company, Pascal Bedward, would design the chemical and biological equipment used in the works and there was a promise of 'no smells'. Plans were approved in

committee in March 1999 and by the full Torbay Council (by 20 votes to 10) in April. There was a great outcry three months later when it was disclosed that the land route from Meadfoot would be used, resulting in much digging and disruption, instead of a possible underwater pipeline across the floor of the Bay.

Work began at Brokenbury at the end of 2000 and continued for several months. The scale of the

A delightful 1960s local press picture of a young girl fishing at Torquay harbour – the picture is also of interest because it shows the Pier Concert Hall, later the Islander Showbar, which spectacularly burned down in 1974.

Major Torquay reconstruction under way in January 1988 as the old Fleet Street and its back alleys disappears in favour of the new Fleet Walk shopping centre.

Torbay Civic Society have in recent years placed a number of Blue Plaques at notable locations around the Three Towns to mark aspects of local history. Pictured here in 2002 is the then Mayor of Torbay, Heather Buckpitt, unveiling the plaque placed at the Palace Hotel, Paignton, to mark its former role as Steartfield House and home of Washington Merritt Singer. The Mayor's Escort, well known hotelier and yachtsman David Buckpitt is fourth from left and in between are Civic Society president Ena Hocking and chairman Ian Handford. The town's first plaques to mark places of interest were instituted by the Rotary Club of Torquay from 1924.

project could be judged from vast piles of rock and soil that dominated the land behind the garage nearest to the building work. By the Spring of 2002 the main task was completed and in March the *Herald Express* reported that four million gallons a day was being treated and a few days later that 'four

treatment operations have been introduced, and high-quality water is being discharged into the sea at Sharkham'. It concluded that 'five million gallons a day of screened water only will continue to be pumped into the sea at Hope's Nose pending the completion of the £6 million pumping station at

The Queen paid a particularly historic visit to Torbay, and to Brixham in particular, in July 1988 to mark the 300th anniversary of the landing of William of Orange, later William III. Complete with umbrella the Queen is shown on a harbour walkabout near the 'King Billy' statue, and unveiling a plaque to commemorate the tercentenary. With her is the then Mayor of Torbay, Denis Reid.

The sign outside Tessier Gardens in St Marychurch, with its controversial 'Adults Only' message. Below: Local historian John Pike pictured in Tessier Gardens for a *Herald Express* story about the origin of the ban on children. This Sun Temple was badly damaged in the storm of 1990 but later repaired.

Ilsham'. Permission to go ahead with this work had taken three years to achieve. Local residents and others contended that the Ilsham Valley playground should be preserved as an open space forever, in view of the restriction placed by the donor, Mr Bazley of Kilmorie, nearly a century ago. Torbay Council at first refused to sell what land was required to SWW and therefore a compulsory purchase order was sought.

Because of possible costs this was not opposed and the order was granted in March 2002. Work started later in the year with the promise that the 'Clean Sweep' programme would be completed before the end of 2004, and all Torbay's effluent

would be passing through the Brokenbury works as planned. When discussions had begun in 1996 the estimate of the cost was £60 million. The actual amount, it seems, will not be much below £100 million – by far the largest amount ever spent on one project in Torbay.

When the *Millennium Story* was completed in 2000 it was published by the *Herald Express* in newspaper-size format only and the comment was made that although each town, Torquay, Paignton and Brixham, had recent histories in bound form, Torbay as a whole lacked a well-bound volume with good illustrations. That situation has now been rectified.

Placenames

Readers are fascinated by the origins of placenames. This is the first time that a full list has been published. The dates of first record are given where this is known.

Anstey's Cove = narrow cove also Anson's, Anstis or Braddy Cove (Anstis quarry 1655).

Ash Hole Cavern, Brixham. Possibly a local name.

Aylescombe and Blatchcombe, possibly after people, Aegel and Blaecci respectively. Ham(m)s were meadows, enclosures, closes. Aliscombe (1644).

Babba[i]combe = Babba's valley (1200).

Barcombe – bearc + hamm = the meadow with the birch trees. Barkham (1641-4); This was still a field-name on 1840 Tithe Map.

Barton = corn farm (OE) = outlying grange.

Bench Bone Cavern, Brixham – at Freshwater Quarry.

Berry Head = dative of OE burg = fort; fortified place.

Blagdon – bloec = the dark hill. Blakedone (1242); Blackdon (1641–4) The manor of Blagdon has a long occupation; the house was probably built by Sir Robert le Denys whose family owned the manors of Collaton and Blagdon. After his sister married Sir Nicholas Kirkham it passed to this family and remained in its hands throughout the 14th, 15th and 16th centuries. It took its name from the nearby hill which was known as Blackdown at least until the 17th century.

Blatchcombe; just a field name in 1840; see Aylescombe.

Beacon Hill, Marldon: site of Armada beacon, looked after by the men of Blackdon'. It had become Blagdon by 1840.

Beacon Hill, Torquay. Known in 19th century as Flagpost Hill. Possibly 'a beacon alow by the water' when manned in 1586.

Braddon = brad (OE) = broad, wide hill.

Brixham = Brioc's ham'? Briseham (1086DB) Brixham (1242 Bk Fees) also Brikesham 1205; Brikkesham 1285.

Brownstone = Bruneston (1242) = Brun's tun.

Cary Park = former name Little Park.

Chapel Hill – Tor Chapel (1793).

Chelston = Ceola's tun? Manor was an ancient parish; part was known as Chilston in 1448; by 1607 it was Cockington and Chilstone'. also Chilson (1438IPM).

Chiseldon Hill = ceosol+dun (OE) = gravel hill. Chiseldon (1842).

Churston = Church tun (1086DB). Hugh de Ferreris held manor in 1303.

Clennon – claene + tun = clean hill (one not covered with woodland?); Cleandon (1641–4).

Cockington = Cocca's tun or cocra (crooked). Chochintona (1086DDB).

Coleton Fishacre = Coletona (1086DB) = Col(l)a's tun, became Fishacre = Egidius de Fyssacre c.1300.

Collaton St Mary – also Colaton Clavil; Collaton Kirkham; Collaton Kirkham otherwise Clavell (1793 sale). Parish church dedicated to St Mary erected 1864–6.

Colley End = Culverhey Strete (1567) = pigeon enclosure.

Combe Pafford (927 Exe.Dioc.) Coombe Pafford (1774 sold under Tithe Redemption Act). Included parts of St Marychurch at time of 1894 Sale).

Copythorne = Coppy Thorne orchard (1842).

Corbyn Head = Corvanesse (1196) = carved nose.

Curledge – earlier Curiditch. (1793 sale).

Daddyhole = Demon (or Daddy)'s Hole.

Daison = Dasey Hill and Dasey Park. (A map of 1770; 1809OS says Dazon. Watkin says that it is a corruption of the Gothic word Daigs making it the place of sacrifice then Black(s) Hill is probably Blag'hill = the sacred way leading to the place of sacrifice. Dazonhill (1849).

Edginswell = Ecgwulf's well or water (1086DB); Eggenswille (1377).

Ellacombe – Allicombe House (1823 Rate Assess.); Ellacombe House (1866OS).

Fernham – fearn = the fern(y) meadow.

Flete = tidal creek or stream. Also Ffleete (1653) Fleete (1711). Becomes New Quay at time of 1803 Act.

Galmpton = tun of the fee-paying men – Galmentona (1086DB). Later variants included: Galmatun (in about 1140), Galmeton (1285), Gampton (1765) and Galmton. (1822).

Gerston – gaers = grass + tun = grassy farm? – lez Garston (1567).

Goodrington – Godrintona in Domesday Book (in the Exchequer copy but not in the Exeter) – indicating the tun of Godhere. Goderington was held by Robert Morcelles Knt. in the time of Henry III. Gorrenton Sands (1667).

Great Hill also Roccombe Hill, Beacon Hill. Likely site of beacon in 16th century. Leased to Admiralty for telegraph, known as Telegraph Hill; sold to owner of Watcombe.

Hele – this could be Hayle in a land sale 1875.

Hollicombe = bohl (OE) + cumb = deep; sunken, hollow; appears as Hollacombe as a field name in 1840.

Hope Farm, Nose, etc. = hop (OE) = (blind) valley. Also known as Bob's Nose (on Trinity House documents and elsewhere).

Ilsham = Illa's ham or from igil = a hedgehog; also: Hylesham, Ylsham, Eylsham, Eylesham, Elsham, Ilesam, among others.

Kent's Cavern = personal name or white cave Kents Hole Close (1659).

Kirkham Street = personal name as Geo. Kyrkeham who held land 1567.

Laywell Spring, Higher Brixham (Polwhele 1797) [Brixham p4].

Lincombe = hlynn (OE) = torrent; clear running water; Linkham (field name).

Livermead = iris or rush meadow, sheltered meadow. Ilifthar Mead; Livermore (1448IPM).

Lupton = Luh(h)a's tun (1086DB).

Lyd Well or Our Lady's Well – a small spring at Wellswood.

Madrepore Road = where the madrepore workers were established. Madrepores were of the genus *caryophyllia* and were found in pebbles on the beach. Blewitt writing in 1832 says: 'The pebbles on the coast are frequently collected by visitors and polished for the madrepores they contain. It is almost unnecessary to say that many unacquainted with the character of organic remains are frequently disappointed in the object of their search, and imagine that every stone must contain a treasure.'

Maidencombe = maegen-dun = maiden or may wood? + cumb; sometimes Mincombe.

Marldon = gentian Mergheldon(e) 14th-century Marldon (1524).

Mearspoole Mead (sale in Paignton 1641–4).

Oar (Ore) stone = grey stone. Horestane (c.1550 Leland).

Oddicombe = oddi (Old Scand.) = point or cape + cumb.

Oldway, Old-Way. Oldway (Directory 1871) also Little Oldway. Old-Way – location 1 mile from Brixham (Memorial to Lord Churston 1858).

Paignton = Paega's tun. Peinton(a) (1086DB); Peyntone (1265); Painton (1215); Paynton (*c*.1630 Risdon). Paington 17th and 18th century + 1837 Harbour Act. also Peinton Key (1644). Paignton from 1833 in Parish Reg, 1867 in Council Minutes.). 30 different spellings.

Penny's Cottages also Beehive Cottages, Rose Cottages (1894 Sale).

Petitor = pytt (OE) = pit, hole, cavity + tor? Could be corruption of Peattle's tor (*cf* Pettiwell).

Philp's Cavern, Brixham. Also Brixham Cavern.

Polhearne = pool + personal name. Polheron (1581SubR).

Preston – earlier Preostatum (the Priest's farm); still vested in the Precentor of Exeter Cathedral [in the 1830s], to whom the great tithes of the parish still belonged by the appropriation of Bishop Quivil.

Quinta = quinta = Sp. villa, country house (1606).

Raddicombe = raefter(OE) beam (place trees, logs from?).

Rae Common – origin doubtful; could be from rá = boundary mark.

Raes Eyes, Brixham – landmark below Rae Common; origin uncertain.

Roundham – ruh = the rough or rugged enclosure. Rowneham (1567).

St Marychurch = Sce Maria circean 1050–72.

Shorton – scir = bright stream. dun (also OE) is a hill or a down.

Smallcombe – smoel = narrow.

Shiphay = sceap (OE) + hay [ham] = sheep enclosure (1086); Coletona (1086DB); Collaton Shephey (1697).

Stantaway Hill – between Teignmouth and Parkfield Roads, possibly stony road fr. OE staniht – stony.

Stentiford's Hill from Wm Stentiford who built two cottages in Pimlico *c*.1810–20; really Appaway Hill. Exploration of cavern found on Happaway Hill Oct. 1862; area now quarried away (behind buildings in Market Street). Also known as Hoppaway as well as Happaway Cavern.

Stoke Gabriel = stoke + dedication of church. Stoke (1307); Stokegabrel (1309); Gabrielstok(e) (14th century) Stoke Sancti Garbrielis (15th century) Stoke Gabriel (1644).

Thatcher – origin uncertain; possibly from OE 'thaec', a covering; on Donn's map 1765 and MacKenzie's Admiralty Survey 1781.

Tor Bay; Torbay = The first printed sea-atlas (or chart) for mariners was drawn in 1584-85 by a Dutchman and reissued in London soon after. This shows the spelling Torbay. The early map of Devon drawn by Christopher Saxton in 1579 also shows it as a single word but on Grenville Collins's sea chart a century later it is written as Tarbay and as a insert in a later one as Tarr Bay. Torbay as a town dates only from 1968 when Torquay, Paignton, Churston and Brixham became a county borough under legislation then in force.

Tormohun (or incorrectly Tormoham but widely used [see below]). Amplifying a brief note in the Exe. Dioc. Arch. Soc. Trans, the vicar of Tor said that the religious vessels used in the 16th century for the Communion were sold for the repair of the quay, writing: 'Hereafter followeth the plate, vestments and jewels and the names of the persons who have taken away the same... one censor of silver, one ship of silver, one oil box of silver, two chalices of silver specified in the last inventory, were sold by the parishioners and the money bestowed by them for the repair of Torr Quay being adjoined to Torr Bay which Quay is a sure and good haven for all ships and boats in time of storm as well as for the interests of the said town.'

Torquay = Torrequay (1591) although a document was addressed to the 'Mayor of Torrekay for the time being'. He was expected to enquire in all manner of treasons, felonies, piracies committed and done upon the sea or in rivers, creakes and portes, the buying of stolen goods and all comforting and abetting of pirates... There was an Addmirall Assize held either in Torquay or Brixham on 27 August; Torkay 1668; Torkey 1715; Tor Quay 1765. la Getie de Torrebaie 1412.

Torre = tor (OE) = high rock, peak or hill. Torra

(1086DB) T(h)orre; Torre Brywere (13th century from Wm Briwere); Torre Moun; Torremohon; Torremohun; Torre Mohoun (14th century) after a daughter of Briwere who married Wm de Mohun. Tormoham was used incorrectly from 1585 to the end of 19th century.

Tor Hill Road = earlier name Church Road.

Totnes Road = Trewe streete = tree street (18–19th century).

Tweenaway = Between the ways (Dartmouth/Newton).

Trumlands = troemel (OE) = monument or cross. Trummerland in 1814.

Upton (Manor) = higher farm.

Waddeton = Wadda's tun (Wadenton 1199); Watton Post (1855 PH).

Waldon Hill (1866OS) = wald (OE) = open/waste ground. (*cf* weald). Also popularly Warren Hill'; possibly rabbit warren for Carys there.

Walls Hill = from prehistoric camp there?

Warborough = waru (OE) + beorg = watch hill; Warberry (field name on TM).

Watcombe = wheat valley. Whatecomb (1414).

Well Street from atte Wille juxta Peynton (1306).

Wellswood = Willswood (field name on Tithe map).

Windmill Hill (or Yaddon Down) as Windmylparke (1580).

Winner Street = Wynerdstrete = vineyard.

Yalberton = alder stream? Aleburne (1242); Yalbourne (1644, 1786).

Torbay timeline

c.AD925	Undated deed establishes the existence of St Marychurch.
1001	Danes in South Devon; villages burned.
1070	Bishop Osbern of Exeter built protecting wall and tower at Paignton; manor held by See of Exeter from about 1050.
1086	Domesday survey.
1196	Torre Abbey founded by monks of the Premonstratensian Order; monks fishing in Torbay.
1224–32	Domesday manor of Ilsham passed to the Abbots of Torre.
1260	Paignton Parish church built, third of site; (first probably Saxon; second Norman built c.1100; present building extensively restored in 19th century.
1295	Market and fair granted to Paignton by Bishop of Exeter for 'three days at the Feast of Holy Trinity'.
1297	Market and fair granted to the manor of Cockington.
1338	Black Prince granted the Waters of Dartmouth (includes Torbay); later part of Duchy of Cornwall.
1373	John Cary purchased the manor of Cockington.
1376	First reference to trawling in national documents.
1557	Manor of Paignton transferred to the Earl of Pembroke; survey made 1567.
1539	Dissolution of Torre Abbey by Henry VIII.
1588	Year of the Spanish Armada; *Nuestra Senora del Rosario* captured; prisoners taken from ship and kept in Tithe Barn at Torre Abbey.
1595	Sir George Cary purchased the manor of St Marychurch.
1609	Sir George Cary endowed almshouses at Cockington (these were removed and rebuilt in 1910)
1654	Mallock family acquire Cockington from the Carys.
1662	Sir George Cary acquired Torre Abbey from John Stowell for £800 (this included a moiety [i.e. a part] of the manor of Tormohun).
1688	William, Prince of Orange, lands at Brixham in November and marches to London where he is proclaimed King William III.
1699	Plan by a Mr Robinson to build a 'mould or harbour' across Torbay.
1739	Manor of Shiphay bought by William Kitson from Sir John Lear of Lindridge.
1768	Manor of Tormohun bought by Robert Palk.
1779	Chapel at Torre Abbey first used (used as a Roman Catholic church until 1859).
1781	Plans for a naval reservoir in the centre of Brixham; built soon after.

1785   Torquay Turnpike Act, improved road to harbour and to Shaldon.

1788   First houses built in the Meadow (beside new turnpike road).

1793   War declared against France; British fleet in Torbay throughout wars until 1815.

1791   More houses being built; called George Street as compliment to Carys.

1796   George Goodridge born at Paignton – a real-life Robinson Crusoe.

1801   Vice-Admiral Lord Nelson at Torre Abbey.

1803   New pier at Torquay; Victoria Parade and Torwood Street built.

1804   Wreck of *HMS Venerable* at Roundham Head; Paignton 'wreckers' at work.

1805   First Ordnance Survey map of the area published.

1806   Cary Parade started.

1808   Miss Pleydell builds house on site of present Torbay Hotel (road terminated there).

1809   Houses built in Swan Street, then called Cane's Lane; replaced older cottages called Cane's Cottages.

1810–11 The Terrace built.

1811   Torquay Bank opened by Messrs Chamberlayne, Saunders and Jefferies.

1814   [Bay Court] Terrace of houses on Park Hill building; completed about 1828 (bombed May 1944).

1815   Napoleon on board *HMS Bellerophon* on his way to St Helena.

1817   Bath House opened with warm and cold sea water baths by Mr Pollard (now Regina Hotel).

c.1820   Livermead House built; first coastal property at Cockington.

  Waldon Hill, a game preserve; development started at about this time.

1820   Market designed by John Foulston built (replaced with new market in 1853).

c.1822   First arrivals of passengers by sea on Portsmouth to Plymouth vessels.

1822   Braddons Hill Road East, Fleet Street and Park Hill being developed. Ballroom designed by John Foulston added to the [Royal] Hotel, [demolished 1993 and awaiting development].

1823   Montpelier Terrace near St John's Church building.

c.1824   Building on the Braddons proceeding (including Braddons Cliff, Braddon Villa and Villa Braganza). Land first advertised in 1809.

1825   Earliest discussion on 'Rail Roads' in Devon.

1825–41 Kent's Cavern explored by Father John McEnery of Torre Abbey.

1826   Torquay National School established in Pimlico. New Turnpike Act and roads constructed to Babbacombe, Shaldon and Newton.

1827   Teignmouth Toll Bridge opened; coastal road improved

1828   Park Place, Union Street (W side) being developed. Mechanics Institute built

1828   "The Spirit of Improvement" in Torquay; *Exeter Flying Post* notes: 'Mr Harvey now has 100 men in his employ'. 5,667 items of mail passing through the Post Office each month; Hearder's Hotel (now the Queen's) opened.

1829–34 Union Street (east side) as far as Market Street built.

c.1830   The Castle built for Mr Luscombe.

1831   Beacon Terrace, Vaughan Parade (the lease dates are earlier), Palk Street, Higher Terrace, Union Hotel built/finished. Floating Bridge (Higher Ferry) over River Dart opened.

1832   Plans drawn up for a railroad from Newton to Torquay (but no action followed).

1833   Princess (later Queen) Victoria landed on quay from yacht *Emerald*.

  Orchard Terrace, Madeira Villa built.

1835 Gasworks opened at top of Torwood Gardens (larger works at Hollacombe, 1861). *Pilmuir* built for Lord Sinclair; Fleete Mill demolished – earliest record of it is in a 1618 deed.

1836 *Marlborough* wrecked off Natural Arch; all on board drowned.

1838 Vomero built (Isambard Kingdom Brunel resident there for a short time); 'Paington Harbour Act' received Royal Assent; first vessels in 1839.

1839 *Torquay Directory* started publication.

1840 Wellswood Hall built for H.C. March Phillips.

c.1841 Waldon Castle built (demolished 1962).

1842 Torbay Road (then New Road, later Station Road) opened under Waldon Hill.

1843 Brixham breakwater started (not completed until 1916); Torwood Grange or Manor demolished

1844–5 99-year leases being granted by L.V. Palk in Lincombes and Warberries [some granted earlier, others later]; Normount (now Bishop's Court) built.

1845 Express trains from Paddington scheduled to reach Exeter in five hours including stops; easily the fastest trains in the world.

Emigration from Torquay harbour in Crossman ships.

1847 Bread riots in Torquay – more serious ones in 1867 when Riot Act read. Isambard Kingdom Brunel bought land at Watcombe for his dream home.

1848 First train arrived at Torquay (then at Torre) Station; journey time from Newton 13 minutes.

1850 First sea road at Meadfoot being built; washed away in 1859; rebuilt with sewer behind sea wall 1877–8; iron mine opened at Torre; building of the Daison commenced.

1851 Lisburne Crescent built; Torquay Cricket Club formed.

1852 Cemetery opened; Western Hospital for Consumptives in Lower Warberry Road established.

c.1853 Terraces in Madrepore Place, Clifton Terrace area building; Local Board rented Public Gardens in Torwood Gardens.

1854 First steeplechases at St Marychurch; they moved to Petitor in 1864.

1856 Abbey Crescent started – builders John Harvey and Richard Henley; Redcliffe Towers built by Colonel Robert Smith.

1857 New Baths opened (later Bath Saloons, etc) Excavation had taken some four years. Dartmouth and Torbay Railway Act received Royal Assent: chief engineer Mr I.K. Brunel.

1858 Windmill Hill Cavern excavations began at Brixham. First sod cut at Torre for the railway line to Kingswear.

1861 Hollacombe Works of the Torquay Gas Company completed; worked until 1968 when North Sea gas arrived.

1864 Sir Lawrence Palk took up residence at new Manor House (now RNIB Rehabilitation Centre).

1865–8 First street to be transformed following establishment of Local Board was Fleet Street, until then narrow, irregular and bounded on either side by small shops and tenements.

1865 *Torquay Times* started publication.

1866 Great hurricane in Torbay (many ships and around 100 lives lost); first Brixham lifeboat, *City of Exeter*, arrived; Imperial Hotel completed.

1867 Torbay Hotel built on site of Marine Villa; Victoria [and Albert] Hotel built; foundation stone of Torquay Harbour (Haldon Pier) laid; opened 1870.

1871 Paignton Bathing Company formed for the accommodation of visitors.

1873 Education Act 1870 adopted at Paignton; a School Board was formed in January 1874.

1873–4   The Wigwam (later Oldway) built by I.M. Singer; altered by son Paris 1904–7.

1874   Torbay House on Paignton sea front demolished (possibly built in the 16th century). Turnpike tolls ended; various tollhouses sold. Paignton Pier Act passed; building did not start until 1878: it finally opened in 1879.

1876–7   Singer trustees built Preston sea wall.

1877   The Fletcher Trust asked by Paignton Local Board to transfer land at Paignton Green. Purchase completed in 1878; layout started in 1879.

1880   Monastery on St Mary's Hill first occupied by the Marist Fathers. Ministry ended there 1984; site subsequently used for lay purposes.

1881   Winter Garden scheme at Torquay started; the cast-iron and glass building was sold to Great Yarmouth 1903 (still in use); Paignton Club built 'in the Classic style'.

1882   Devon County Agricultural Show held at Cockington.

1883   St Marychurch Town Hall opened (designed by G.S. Bridgman, the man who built the Wigwam); wing added 1886.

1885   Shiphay Manor rebuilding completed. Lord Haldon Estates Act received Royal Assent. John Henry Lee 'hanged three times' for the murder of Miss Keyse at Babbacombe Glen – commuted to life imprisonment, released in 1907.

1886   Haldon Pier bought by Torquay Local Board.

1889   Permission given to prospect for gold on Daddyhole Plain. Recreation Ground near Torquay Station opened. Thomas Adams bought LIFU steam bus – ran between Torquay and Paignton.

1892   Torquay's Charter of Incorporation received in September.

1893   Torquay Town Association became Torquay and District Chamber of Commerce; Council decided to build a 'promenade pier'. Dr Paget Blake offers curios collection to Borough. Royal Terrace Gardens opened by the Mayor of Torquay.

1894   Cockington Local Board elected. Public park at St Marychurch given by R.S.S. Cary; Princess Gardens opened by the Mayor.

1895   Princess Pier opened informally.

1896   St Marychurch Local Board first rented a cottage at Lawes Bridge as an infectious hospital. Tottiford and Kennick watersheds bought for £40,000.

1898   Electricity first supplied from power station on Beacon Quay.

1900   St Marychurch and Cockington (ie Chelston) incorporated into the Borough of Torquay. Filling of marshes and layout of Queen's Park, Paignton commenced. Venford reservoir on Dartmoor being built for Paignton Council. In October mixed bathing was allowed at Meadfoot for the first time.

1901   Queen's Park at Paignton opened. Foundation stone laid on the Strand of Clock Tower to be built as a memorial to Richard Mallock.

1903   Torquay Winter Garden sold to Great Yarmouth Corporation for £1,300. Kents Cavern sold; still in family's hands. Steam bus service inaugurated.

1904   Berry Head lighthouse built. Motor omnibus service started by GWR between Paignton and Torquay.

1905   Bye-law approved; all vehicles to show lights at night. Torquay Tramway Company began building a tramway at Torre.

1907   Tramway service started in Torquay; 23,409 passengers carried in first five days. Extended to Paignton in 1911. Trenchford reservoir completed with a capacity of 171 million gallons. First public library opened in Torquay (new building in Lymington Road 1938).

1910   Halley's Comet seen in Torbay; Review in

Torbay of Fleet by King George V; Claude Grahame-White made historic flight over ships. Tramway service extended to Paignton. Road signs introduced at Paignton.

1912 Torquay Pavilion opened; first performance by Torquay Municipal Orchestra (disbanded 1953). Ceased to be a theatre in 1974.

1913 Town Hall at Castle Circus completed. Centenary Regatta celebrated.

1914 War declared against Germany; Austrians and Germans in Torbay arrested; first wounded soldiers arrived in Torbay, later visited by Queen Mary. Seaplane base in Torquay harbour.

1915 Torquay Secondary (later Grammar) school for boys and girls opened. King George V and Queen Mary visited war hospitals.

1916 German U-boat attacked Brixham fleet, trawlers *Provident* and *Amphitrite* sunk.

1917 New Zealand wounded arrived and quartered in St Marychurch.

1918 Armistice signed; no official celebrations took place. Influenza epidemic killed many.

1919 Cairn's Torquay film studio opened at Watcombe (first film 1920). Paignton Pierhead burned down. Ministry of Transport formed; 'A' and 'B' roads designated.

1920 Former German warships aground at Paignton; local coastguards rewarded. First Merryweather motor fire engine bought. Council houses being built at Westhill.

1921 Torquay Cenotaph dedicated (list of 596 names of war casualties).

1922 Inspection by King George V of Fleet in Torbay. Goodrington Cottage bought for development by Paignton Council. North end of Preston Green acquired as an open space.

1923 Primley Zoological Gardens founded by Herbert Whitley.

1924 Mrs Rowcroft gave £8,000 to buy Hengrave as site for new hospital. Marine Drive opened – work carried out by the unemployed. Abbey Park and Gardens at Torquay opened.

1925 Skull between 15,000 and 20,000 years old found at Kents Cavern. *Torbay Herald and Express* started publication.

1926 Hele housing estate started on 36 acres of land bought from the Cary Estate. Babbacombe Cliff Railway opened for the first time.

1927 Great Hill reservoir opened. Torquay United AFC made its debut in the Football League. White lines on roads introduced. Westhill School opened (new Westlands School 2002).

1928–9 Carillon installed at All Saints' Church, Brixham; played tunes of Lyte's famous hymns since.

1930 Torre Abbey and its lands purchased by Borough for £40,000. New Torbay Hospital opened by Edward, Prince of Wales.

1931 Completion of Cliff Gardens and Promenade at Roundham Head, Paignton.

1932 The Regent Cinema in Paignton officially opened in August; Palladium shortly afterwards. Pedestrian crossings introduced at Paignton.

1933 Cockington Court and 223 acres of land leased to Borough for 999 years by Cockington Trust; freehold subsequently bought for £50,000.

1934 Last trams ran in Torquay and Paignton. Road Traffic Act introduced 30 mph speed limit.

1935 Paignton sewerage scheme completed with outfall at Sharkham, Brixham.

1936 Drum Inn at Cockington opened, Designed and furnished by Sir Edwin Lutyens. Paignton Harbour acquired by the Council from Paignton Harbour Co. Last visit of J-Class yachts.

1937 King George V Memorial playing fields opened at Watcombe.

1938   Audley Park School built in Cricketfield Road, Torquay.

1939   Municipal house building started at Combe Pafford, Watcombe (completed after World War Two).

1939   World War Two begins; coastal batteries built at Brixham and Kingswear.

1940   Machine-gun posts and pill-boxes erected; Paignton Pier isolated from shore. All road signs removed. Local Defence Volunteers (later the Home Guard) formed (stood down 3 December 1944). Large number of Belgian refugees arrived by sea at Brixham.

1942   'Cat's eyes' introduced on Torbay's roads. RAF hospital at Palace Hotel bombed by German bombers; second direct hit in 1943. Morrison and Anderson shelters arrived and distributed.

1942   Rogation Sunday air-raid on St Marychurch parish church, many children killed.

1944   Preparations for D-Day: Torbay included in Protected Area. Many US troops billeted in Torbay towns; convoys sailed from Torbay.

1946   *Western Lady* ferry service started operations. Oldway purchased by Paignton UDC. Village of Cockington bought by Prudential; further sale in 1964. Torre churchyard tombstones removed and became a garden of rest; dedicated in July 1947.

1948   XIV Olympiad yachting events held in Torbay.

1949   Gallowsgate reservoir completed.

1950   International conference leading to General Agreement on Tariffs and Trade; ended January 1951.

1955   Herbert Whitley died, zoo subsequently controlled by Herbert Whitley Trust. Bishop of Exeter creates new parish of Shiphay. Shiphay Church, built on site of Church Hall, opened.

1956   First Tall Ships Race from Torbay to Lisbon. *Mayflower II* launched at Upham's yard, Brixham.

1959   British Dental Association Conference held in Torquay.

1960   Court House built on site of old Upton School. Kilmorie demolished (new flats built in 1962). British Medical Association Conference held in Torquay.

1961   Torquay Princess Theatre opened. Conference of European Postal and Telecommunications Administrations took place in Torquay. Special commemorative stamps issued.

1963   Model Village constructed at St Marychurch by Tom Dobbins. Brixham branch line closed by British Rail; track subsequently removed. Kitson Park at Shiphay opened.

1967   Paignton Festival Theatre opened.

1968   Torquay joined Paignton, Churston and Brixham to become the County Borough of Torbay. New Roman Catholic Church at Brixham completed with a car park on its roof.

1969   YMCA youth centre opened at Clennon Valley by Queen Mother. Queen's visit to the Western Fleet.

1970   Demolition of Marine Spa.

1971   New fish market and jetty opened at Brixham. New overbridge at Torbay Road completed.

1972   Paignton-Kingswear railway line taken over by Dart Valley Railway Company.

1973   Development at Broadsands Beach including new café.

1974   Reorganisation of local government nationally. Torbay lost County Borough status. Some services passed to Devon CC; water and sewerage to SWWA; some health services to THA. Oldway remained Torbay Council Chamber.

1976   Torquay Central Church completed at a cost about £500,000.

1977   Coral Island (leased by Torbay Borough) opened; cost £1.5 million.

1984   Torquay Marina begun; Haldon Centre, now Union Square, completed.

1986   Paignton celebrated 900-year history – based on entry in Domesday Book.

1987   English Riviera Centre opened on site of Rosetor and Roselea. Fleet Walk project started with demolition of part of Fleet Street; completed 1990 including pedestrianisation.

1988   Tercentenary of landing of William of Orange; visit by HM the Queen to Torbay: Quaywest leisure complex opened at Goodrington: Brixham Marina started building.

1990   Severe gale with 100 mph winds; Brunel Woods, Warberry Copse and many other parts of Torbay suffered tree losses.

1991   Riviera Way and Sainsbury's new store opened.

1998   Unitary Authority created.

1999   Apollo multi-screen complex opened at Paignton. Laser World & European Qualifying Regatta held in Torbay.

2000   New toilets and booking office opened in Abbey Park replacing those destroyed by vandals.

2001   *Carnival Pride* called in Torbay on way from Finland to the Caribbean.

2002   Around Alone yacht race had stop-over at Brixham. Redevelopment of Beacon Hill and Harbour started; completed 2003.

Bibliography

No volume on Torbay can be complete without giving its readers the opportunity to read further. One of my objectives when writing the Torbay Heritage Series (listed below) was to include in each volume a complete list of all the relevant books and articles in periodicals. These, therefore, are not reprinted here. The titles below have been chosen to give useful 'words and pictures' stories about the three towns. Out of print items may be borrowed through local libraries.

Torbay

Bainbridge, B. *Around Torbay* 2000.

Barham, F. *Torbay Transport* 1979.

Born, A. *Torbay Towns* 1990.

Cockington Coast and Countryside Trust. *The South West Coast Path through Torbay: a Guide to its Route, History and Wildlife* 2000

Pannell, N. *Tor Bay; the History and Wildlife of Torbay's Dramatic Coastline* 1998.

Pearce, F. *The Book of Torbay: a Century of Celebration* 1999

Pike, J.R. *Tall ships in Torbay: a Maritime History* 986.

Poole, Keith. ed. *The Art of the Torquay and South Devon Potteries* 996.

Potts, C.R. *The Kingswear Branch* 1990.

Torquay

Ellis, A.C. *Historical Survey of Torquay* 1930.

Holgate, M. *Torquay*. 1999.

Holgate, M. *Devon Derbies, 1920-2001. (Football matches between Torquay, Exeter and Plymouth AFCs)* 2002.

Kelland, John. *Shiphay Collaton; its Church, its Times, its People* 1997.

Pateman, L.L. *Pictorial and Historical Survey of Babbacombe and St Marychurch* 2v 1980; 1991.

Pearce, F. *Marine Spa* 2000

Pike, J.R. *Torquay: The Place and the People, 1892–1992* 1992.

Pike, J.R. *Torquay: a Photographic History of Your Town*, 2001

Pike, J.R. *Torquay. Torbay's Heritage series* 1994.

Read, B. *Cockington*. (pt.1 1999; pt.2 2000).

Russell, P. *A History of Torquay* 1960.

Seymour, D. *Torre Abbey* 1977.

Thomas, D. and E. Lloyd. *The Old Torquay Potteries* 1977.

Torbay Council. *Torre Abbey*. [2000].

Paignton

Brandon, R. *Singer and the Sewing Machine*.

Parnell, P. *Paignton* 2002.

Pearce, F. *A Book of Paignton* 2001.

Pike, J.R. *Paignton. Torbay's Heritage series* 1993

Pike, J.R. and Torquay Natural History Society. comps. *Paignton* 1997.

Tully, P. *Pictures of Paignton*. 3 parts 1988-95

Brixham

Corin, J. *'Provident' and the story of the Brixham smacks* 1980.

Ellis, A.C. *History of Brixham*; transcribed and ed. by D. Wilson 1992.

Gosling, T. *Brixham* 1996.

Johnson, D. *Landing of William of Orange, 1688* 1988.

Pearce, F. *Book of Brixham: portrait of a harbour town* 2000

Pike, J.R. *Brixham. Torbay's Heritage Series* 1993

Potts, C.R. *The Brixham Branch*. 1986.

Salsbury, A. *A History of the Torbay Lifeboats* 2002

Index

The entries listed in the Chronology are not included in this index.